Maritime English Communications based on
Standard Maritime Communication Practice

항해실무영어

박진수 · 김성준 엮음

글터
GEUL TER

- 차 례 -

I. Log Book

II. Standard Marine Navigation Vocabulary

III. Standard Maritime Communication Practice

I

Log Book

1. 항해일지

1.1 Log book의 어원

영어의 log(통나무)에서 유래했는데, log 자체의 어원은 불분명하다. SOED에는 앵글로 라틴어의 loggiare(나무토막으로 베다)와 loggum (통나무) 등의 낱말이 1205년과 1306년에 사용된 용례가 있음을 밝히고 있다[1]

'나무'(log)가 선박운항에서 가장 중요한 **일지, 선속, 항정, 항정계**를 모두 포괄하게 되었다는 것은 매우 재미있는 주제다. 시대적으로 본다면, log는 **log-board(logbook, 항해일지)** → **chip-log(선속측정기)** → **log(항정계)** 등의 순서로 해사용어로 전화된 것으로 보인다. 유럽의 항해가들은 항해 중 중요한 지점을 통과했거나, 암초나 얕은 해역 등을 만나게 되면 이를 기록해두는 관행이 있었다. 15세기 포르투갈과 스페인의 항해가들이 이와 같은 기록을 상세하게 기록했고, 콜럼버스는 1492년 1차 항해 때 항해일지를 매우 충실하게 작성하기도 했다. 16세부터 18세기에 이르기까지 유럽의 뱃사람들은 당직 중 얼마나 항해했는지를 파악할 수 있도록 나무 판(log-board)에 표로 만들어 놓고 여기에 기입했다. log-board는 위도, 침로, 항해거리, 풍향과 풍속, 나침반의 자차와 편차 등을 일목요연하게 표로 만들어 놓은 흑판(blackboard)이었다. 17세기 후반에 log-board가 종이에 인쇄되어 책으로 묶여 나오게 되면서 log-book이라고 부르게 되었고,[2] 1825년 즈음에는 간단히 log라고 부르기에 이르렀다.[3]

---

1) *The Shorter Oxford English Dictionary*, p.1232.
2) J.B. Hewson, *A History of the Practice of Navigation*, pp.172-176.
3) *The Shorter Oxford English Dictionary*, p.1232.

Monthes and daies of the month.	Latitude G.	M.	Corse	Leages	Winde	The 23 of March, Cape S. Augustine in Brasill being 16 leags east from me, I began this accopt.
March 24	7	30	N.N.E.	25	East	
25	5	44	N. by E., norly	36	Eb.N.	Compasse varied 9 deg. the South point westward.
26	4	1	N. by N. (?)	35	E.b.N.	Compasse varied 8 deg. the South point westward.
27	2	49	N.	24	E. × N.	
28	1	31	N. easterly	26	E. × N.	
29	1	4	N.N.W.	9	N.E.	Compasse varied 6 deg. 40m the South point westward.
31	0	0	N.b.W.	21	E.N.E.	Observation, the Pole above the Horizon.

log-board of 1593 in John Davis' *The Seaman's Secrets*(1594)[4]

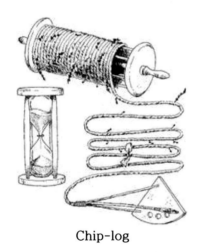

Chip-log

- 속력 단위 : knot

† long glass(28초)
- knot 47ft 3inch(14.402m)

† short glass(14초)
- knot 23ft 7.7inch(7.2m)

1.2 Log Book의 중요성

1) 선박 운항상 중요한 참고자료
2) 항해기술이나 화물의 선적이나 관리의 적절성을 판정하는 자료
3) 해양사고가 발생할 경우 사고 원인을 규명하는 자료가 되며, 해양사고 심판시 제1 증거 서류가 된다.
4) 선장과 당직사관의 직무의 적절성을 판정하는 자료가 되어 선주

---

4) Hewson, *A History of the Practice of Navigation*, p.172.

와 선장, 당직사관의 이익을 보호할 수 있다.
5) 법률상 중요한 증거 서류

2. Log Book의 기록

2.1 Log Book 기재상의 일반적 주의 사항

1) 선장, 당직사관의 직무 수행을 성실히 수행했음을 입증하는 중요한 서류라는 사실을 염두에 두어야 한다.
2) 연필로 기록해서는 안되며, 반드시 볼펜이나 만년필로 기록해야 한다. **한번 기록한 것은 지워서는 안된다.**
3) 잘못 기재한 내용은 **틀린 부분에 줄을 긋고, 정정**해야 한다.
4) 기사는 간단하고 명확한 표현을 사용해야 한다.
5) 일이 발생한 뒤에 기록한 것이므로 **과거형**을 사용해야 한다.
6) **중요한 사항**, 특히 해양사고와 관련해서는 기록하기 전에 **선장과 반드시 상의 후 기록**해야 한다.

2.2 Log Book 영문의 특징

1) 주어(Our Vessel, She, We, Captain)의 생략
보기) (The Vessel 생략) Left Busan for Long Beach.
    (Captain 생략) Mustered <u>all hands</u> on deck.
2) Be 동사의 생략
보기) Vessel (was 생략) easy in slight sea and low avg. NW'ly
        swell.
    All precautions (were 생략) observed.
3) 정관사 The의 생략 : 바다, 하천, 선박, 군도 등에 The를 붙이지 않는다.
보기) the Pacific Ocean → Pacific Ocean
    the Panama Canal → Panama Canal
    the Thames → Thames
    the Rigel → Rigel

4) 핵심 낱말을 제외하고 생략할 수 있다.

보기) Rung S.B.E. → S.B.E. or S/B Eng.

　　　(It was) fine and clear. → Fine and clear.

　　　(We sent the) first line. → First line.

5) 과거 시제로 쓴다.

보기) Inspected all cargo holds and deck lashings.

　　　Secured from fire−fighting drill.

6) 약자나 기호를 애용한다.

보기) starboard → STB'D, STBD, stb

　　　port side → P/S

　　　Container → Cont. or CU=container unit

7) 항해전문용어를 사용한다.

보기) made out : 초인(初認)하다

　　　turned to : 일을 시작하다

3. Log Book의 기사란의 기재

3.1 기상

·Fine and clear. Rolling easily in slight NE'ly swell.

　청명한 날씨. 북서 방향에서의 약한 너울에 약하게 옆질(橫搖)함.

·VSL steaming easily and steady with very little rolling & pitching motion.

　약간 옆질과 앞뒷질(從搖)을 하며 순항 중

·Vessel rolling heavily in a confused swell and pitching and yawing easily. Some light rain. Weather seems to be abating.

　일정하지 않는 너울을 받으며, 심한 옆질(횡요)을 하고, 쉽사리 앞뒷질(종요)와 요잉을 함. 약간 비가 내림. 날씨가 점차 개이고 있음.

　·Vessel rolling gently in moderating NE sea & winds. Sky partly cloudy. Vis. good. No traffic.

　북동쪽으로부터 상당한 파도와 바람을 받으며, 부드럽게 옆질 함. 하늘에는 부분적으로 구름이 끼어 있고, 시정은 좋으며, 선박 통항

이 없었음.

· Weather increasing in intensity. Snow flurries. Barometer falling.

　기상이 점점 험악해지고, 눈이 휘날리며, 기압이 떨어짐.

· Decreased speed to 90 RPM to ease the vessel in rough weather.

　거친 날씨에 배의 동요를 줄이기 위해 기관회전수를 90으로 줄임.

· Vis. fair with occasional flurries. Wind veering to NNW & mod. NNW sea.

　이따금 눈이 날리고, 시정은 좋음. 풍향이 북북서로 바뀌고 있으며, 북북서 방향의 파도가 상당함.

· O'cast, passing snow, vis. good to fair in snow. Vessel pitching & rolling heavily at times in a very high seas & heavy swells.

　구름이 잔뜩 끼어 있고, 눈이 지나감. 눈이 내리나 시정은 양호함. 매우 높은 파도와 심한 너울 속에 때로 옆질과 앞뒷질을 심하게 함.

· Laboured heavily, shipping seas on deck frequently.

　심하게 흔들리고, 갑판에 해수가 자주 올라옴.

· Vessel taking occasional seas on deck port side from rough beam seas(SW'ly) and high short swell.

　거친 횡파(남서쪽)와 높고 짧은 너울을 받아 이따금 갑판 좌현 측에 해수가 올라옴.

· Received several very high swells on port beam. Ship rolled to max. 34°, C/Co. to 345° pgc(Per Gyro Compass) to get out of heavy roll.

　좌현 횡방향에서 수 차례 매우 높은 너울을 받았다. 최대 34도까지 옆질을 함. 심한 옆질에서 벗어나기 위해 자이로 침로 345°로 변침함.

3.2 견시 및 순시

· Kept a sharp look-out through the watch.
당직 중 엄중하게 견시함.

· Fog conditions prevailed. S.B.E.(S/B eng.) Visibility reduced A/C(according to) fog. All precautions observed. Radar on(or monitored).
안개가 낌. 기관 사용 준비. 안개로 시정이 축소됨. 제반 주의를 기함. 레이더 작동함.

· Fog lookout on bow. All regulations observed.
선수에 무중 견시 배치함. 모든 규정을 준수함.

· Round made all in ACC.(accommodation)/ E/R(engine room) area for fire, safety and security.
선실과 기관실 구역에 화재, 안전, 보안 점검차 순시함.

· Fog lifted (cleared) and Full ahead.
안개가 걷히고 기관 전속 전진.

3.3 주요 물표 항과 및 정침

· Passed Ulgi L.H. on 280°, 2 miles off and set course(S/Co) on 245°.
울기등대를 280도, 2마일 떨어져 항과(航過)한 뒤 245도로 정침

· Set course 177° G & T, 175° ST(Standard Magnetic Compass) with Billings Head L.H. 1.5 M/O(miles off)
Billings Head 등대를 1.5 마일 떨어져 자이로침로와 진침로 177도, 표준나침의 침로 175도로 정침함

· Hongdo abeam port side, 3.5 miles off. C/Co(changed course) to 270° T & G. 275° S.
홍도를 좌현 정횡, 3.5 마일 떨어져 항과함. 진침로와 자이로침로 270도, 표준나침의 275도로 변침함.

3.4 선내 시계

· Retarded(Advanced) clocks 1 hour to ZD(zone description) +9.

　+9 시간대에 맞추기 위해 선내 시간을 1시간 후진함(전진함).

· Put ship's clocks 30 minutes ahead(back) for UTC(coordinated universal time) +5.

　협정세계시 +5에 맞추기 위해 선내 시간을 30분 전진함(후진함).

3.5 이로(離路, deviation)

· As per instruction from Seoul Head Office, altered course to 245° T and proceeded to Saigon.

　서울 본사로부터의 지시에 따라, 진침로 245도 변침하여 사이공으로 항진함.

· Altered course and proceeded for the rescue of the ship in distress, and answered the distress signals from that ship.

　조난선을 구조하기 위해 변침하여 항진함. 조난선으로부터 조난신호에 응답함.

3.6 점검 및 시험

· Tested general alarm, whistles, navigation lights, telegraph. All in order. Changed over port steering pump to STB'D.

　경보기, 기적, 항해등, 텔레그래프를 시험함. 모두 이상 없음. 좌현 조타 펌프를 우현 조타펌프로 변경.

· Inspected all cargo holds and deck lashings. Took temperatures as per left. All found in good order.

　화물창과 갑판 고박(固搏) 상태를 점검함. 왼쪽에 기재한 것과 같이 온도를 측정함. 모두 양호함.

· Completed check of cargo holds, found : #2 U/TD(upper Tween deck)-11 units pulp down, #2 L/TD(lower TD)-11 rolls paper down, #4 U/TD-approx. 90 bales pulp down, #6

U/TD-9 bales pulp tumbled. Unable to enter #1 P/S(port side) FWD(forward) locker.

화물창 검사를 마침. 다음과 같은 이상이 발견됨. 2번창 상부 중갑판 펄프 11 단위가 내려 앉음. 2번창 하부 중갑판 - 종이 11 뭉치가 내려 앉음. 4번창 상부 중갑판 - 펄프 약 90포가 내려 앉음. 6번창 상부 중갑판 펄프 9포가 굴러 떨어짐. 1번창 좌현 전부 격납고에는 진입 불가.

· Completed visual inspection of cargo gear. All falls, topping lifts, rings, shackles, swivels, hooks, booms, blocks, fairleads & winches found to be in good working condition.

하역 장치에 대한 육안 검사를 실시함. 폴, 토핑 리프트, 링, 쉐클, 스위벌, 후크, 붐, 블록, 페어리드, 윈치 등이 양호함.

· Master and Dept. heads conducted sanitary inspection of crew quarters, galley, mess room area, and public toilets. General condition satisfactory. Deficiencies notes and duly remedied.

선장과 각 직장이 거주구역, 취사실, 사관식당, 공용 화장실에 대한 위생 점검을 실시함. 전반적으로 양호하나, 발견된 결함은 적절히 시정됨.

· Closed all watertight openings and tested the water tightness. All found in good order.

수밀 개구를 모두 닫고, 수밀 검사결과 양호함.

3.7 훈련

· Exercised boat station drill, inspected the boat equipment and ensured that all's in apparent good order.

단정 부서 훈련 실시함. 의장품을 점검. 외관상 모두 양호함.

· Practised fire station drill and inspected the fire-fighting appliances. All found in good order.

소화 훈련을 실시하고 소방비품을 점검함. 상태 양호.

·Mustered all hands on boat deck and inspected that they were suitably clad and put on their life jackets in a proper manner.

전 선원을 단정 갑판에 소집하고, 착의 및 구명동의 착용의 적절성에 대해 점검함.

·Held fire & boat drill in Lat. 42° 00′ N, Long. 165°15′ W. 1300: Sounded fire alarm. 6 hoses led(pulled) out & full pressure applied. Emergency transmitter, emergency generator & W/T(water tight) doors operated. 1320: Sounded abandon ship. All crew members and passengers mustered at their stations and instructed. Boats lowered to sea level & raised. Propelling gear operated and instructed ahead & astern. 1345: Secured from drills. All equipment in apparent good condition.

북위 42도 00분, 서경 165도 15분 해역에서 소화 및 단정훈련 실시. 1300 : 화재 경보 발령. 소화 호스 6개를 인출하여 전 압력을 가함. 비상송신기, 비상발전기, 수밀문 작동함. 1320 : 퇴선신호 발령. 승무원 및 여객 전원 퇴선 위치에 소집하고 교육 실시. 단정을 내리고 올림. 수동추진장치를 전후로 작동함. 1345: 훈련 해제함. 의장품 외관상 모두 양호함.

3.8 정박 중

·Anchor bearing checked. No movement of vessel observed.
투표 방위 점검함. 본선 이동 없음.

·Routine rounds of inspections made of lights, lines, and gangway. All in good order.
등화, 계류색, 현문 순시함. 이상 없음.

·Commenced heaving in anchor to shift to N-4 anchorage.
N-4 묘지로 전선하기 위해 닻을 감아올리기 시작함.

·Completed hauling ship. Vessel in position.
전선을 완료하고 선박 제 위치.

· Quarantine officer aboard to inspect all around ship.
　검역관이 승선해 선내 모두를 점검함.
· Started fumigation for the destruction of vermin and roddents by the employment of hydrocyanic acid gas.
　해충 및 설치 동물 족의 구제를 위해 청산가스로 훈증소독 실시함.

· Surveyors aboard for loading and discharging liquid cargo.
　액화 화물 선적 및 양하를 위해 검사원 승선
· USCG inspector Lt.(lieutenant) F.W. Ringsage on board. Inspected W.T. door repair at Fr. # 137 STB'D side and all manual and remoter controls to all W.T. doors. All found in good condition.
미 해안경비대 링사지 대위 승선. 프레임 137번 우측 수밀문의 수리와 수밀 전부의 수동 및 원격 조정 상태 점검함. 모두 양호.

· ABS(American Bureau of Shipping) tested and passed as satisfactory the repair by welding to opening in shell plating, plate G-6, frame 48.
　미국선급에서 프레임 48 철판 G-6에 있는 개구부의 용접수리를 시험하여 양호한 것으로 판정함.

· Lifted all derrick booms up in preparation for loading cargo.
　선적준비를 위해 데릭 붐을 모두 올림.
· Crew rigged heavy derricks aloft and opened hatch covers.
　선원들이 헤비 데릭을 리깅하고 해치 커버를 개방함.

· 6 Gangs of longshoremen came on board and commenced loading cargo at Nos. 1, 2, 3, & 5 hatches.
　하역인부 6개조가 승선하여 1, 2, 3, 5번 해치의 선적을 시작함.
· Stopped cargo work owing to(due to) passing shower.
　지나가는 비로 인해 하역작업 일시 중지함.

· Resumed cargo work.
  하역작업 재개함.
· Finished loading cargo at No. 3 hold.
  3번 화물창의 선적 작업 완료.
· Lowered all derrick booms and battened all hatched down.
  모든 데릭 붐을 내리고, 해치를 모두 덮고 고박함.

3.9 사고

· Soundings of all tanks and bilges disclosed no evidence of leakage.
  탱크와 빌지 측심 결과 누수 없음.

· While the vessel was proceeding at full speed, she struck bottom and afterwards moved straight ahead for approx. 200 yards and stopped hard aground.
  본선은 전속으로 항진 중 해저와 접촉한 뒤 약 200야드 전진해 정지함.
· Divers report indicated no evidence of underwater damage and that vessel's bottom was resting full length on a firm hard clay bottom formation.
  잠수사의 보고에 따르면, 해면하 손상의 흔적은 없으며, 선저는 단단하고 굳은 진흙 해저에 전체가 얹혀 있다고 함.
· Vessel's crew proceeding to pump ballast from tanks with the view to attempting to refloat the vessel at next high tide 1100 hrs on July 30.
  다음 고조시에 배의 부양을 시도할 목적으로 본선 선원들은 계속해 밸러스트를 배출함.
· Ship being in danger of striking on a rock by strong gale, got ship run on shore intentionally.(Lat. 10° 30′N, Long. 150° 10′W)
  강풍으로 인해 암초에 부딪힐 위험이 있어 자의로 해안에 좌주시킴.(북위 10° 30′, 서경 150° 10′)

· Collided with an American freighter MV Golden Steel with her STB'D bow, causing damage of smashing handrail on the forecastle. No injury to crew and cargo and proceeded on her voyage.

본선은 미국 화물선 골든 스틸 호와 우현 선수가 충돌하여 핸드 레일이 파손됨. 인명 및 적하 피해는 없었으며 항진을 계속함.

· Struck against a fishing boat which carried no lights. Stopped engine immediately to pick up the fishermen of the crushed boat.

등화를 켜지 않은 어선을 충돌함. 즉시 기관을 정지시키고 박살난 어선에서 입수한 어부들을 구조함.

· Touched with submerged substance and was unfortunately holed in No.1 hold.

수중 장애물과 접촉해 불행히도 1번창에 파공이 생김.

· Placed the collision mat right over the leak with the assistance of the diver.

잠수부의 도움을 받아 침수되는 곳의 바로 위에 방수 매트를 설치함.

· While paying out port cable, it parted at 4th shot. Immediately cast anchor buoy to indicate the spot of the lost anchor and cable.

묘쇄를 신출하던 중 4절이 끊어짐. 잃어버린 묘 및 묘쇄의 위치를 표시해두기 위해 즉시 앵커 부이를 던짐.

· On account of a sudden trouble with the steering gear, ran against with a crossing fishing boat.

조타 장치의 돌연한 고장으로 횡단하는 어선과 충돌함.

II Standard Marine Navigation Vocabulary

IMO Standard Marine[5) Communication Phrases
[IMO Res.A.918(22)]

GLOSSARY

The GLOSSARY also includes a limited number of technical terms which do not appear in the text of the SMCP, but might be useful in case the content of a given standard Phrase requires modification.

1   General terms

Abandon vessel	To evacuate crew and passengers from a vessel following a distress
Accommodation ladder	Ladder attached to platform at vessel's side with flat steps and handrails enabling persons to embark / disembark from water or shore
Adrift	Floating, not controlled, without a clearly determinable direction
Air draft	The height from the waterline to the highest point of the vessel
Assembly station	Place on deck, in mess rooms, etc., assigned to crew and passengers where they have to meet according to the muster list when the corresponding alarm is released or announcement made
Backing (of wind)	Shift of wind direction in an anticlockwise manner, for example from north to west. opposite of veering

---

5) **marine** : 라틴어의 '바다'를 뜻하는 *mare*(여성형), *marinus*(남성형)에서 유래한 낱말로 고대 프랑스어 marin(여성형 marine)을 거쳐 영어에 유입되었다. SOED에 따르면, '바다의'(connected with the sea)의 의미로는 1551년, 상선대(the shipping, fleet) 등의 의미로는 1669년, '해병'의 의미로는 1690년에 각각 사용된 첫 용례가 문헌적으로 확인되고 있다. 유럽의 주요 언어에서 '바다'와 관련된 단어는 노르만어에서 유래한 sea와 라틴어의 mare로 구별되는데, 명사는 sea로, 형용사는 주로 mare에서 유래한 marine이나 maritime이 사용되고 있다. 김성준, 『해사영어의 어원』, p.339.

Beach (to)	To run a vessel up on a beach to prevent its sinking in deep water
Berth	1: A sea room to be kept for safety around a vessel, rock, platform, etc.. 2: The place assigned to a vessel when anchored or lying alongside a pier, etc.
Blast	A sound signal made with the whistle of VSL
Blind sectors	Areas which cannot be scanned by the radar of the vessel because they are shielded by parts of its superstructure, masts, etc, or shore obstructions.
Boarding arrangements	All equipment, such as pilot ladder, accommodation ladder, hoist, etc., necessary for a safe transfer of the pilot
Boarding speed	The speed of a vessel adjusted to that of a pilot boat at which the pilot can safely embark / disembark
Bob-cat	A mini-caterpillar with push-blade used for the careful distribution of loose goods in cargo holds of bulk carriers
Briefing	Concise explanatory information to crew and/or passengers
Cable	1: Chain, wire or rope connecting a vessel to her anchor(s) 2: (measurement), 185.2 metres, i.e. one tenth of a nautical mile
Capsizing	Turning of a vessel upside down while on water
Cardinal buoy	A seamark, i.e. a buoy, indicating the North, East, South or West, i.e. the cardinal points from a fixed point. such as a wreck, shallow water, banks, etc.

Cardinal points	The four main points of the compass, i.e. North, East, South and West; for the purpose of the SMCP the intercardinal points, i.e. Northeast, Southeast, etc., are also included
Casualty	here: Case of death in an accident or shipping disaster
Check (to)	1: To make sure that equipment etc. is in proper condition or that everything is correct and safe 2: To regulate motion of a cable, rope or wire when it is running out too fast
Close-coupled towing	A method of towing vessels through polar ice by means of icebreaking tugs with a special stern notch suited to receive and hold the bow of the vessel to be towed
Close up (to)	To decrease the distance to the vessel ahead by increasing one`s own speed
Compatibility(of goods)	states whether different goods can be stowed together in one hold
Constrained	A vessel severely restricted by her draft in her ability to (Vessel constrained by deviate from the course followed in relation to the available her draft) depth and width of navigable water.
Convoy	A group of vessels which sail together, e.g. through a canal or ice
Course	The intended direction of movement of a vessel through the water
Course made good	That course which a vessel makes good over ground, after allowing for the effect of currents, tidal streams, and leeway caused by wind and sea
COW	Crude Oil Washing: A system of cleaning the cargo tanks by washing them with the cargo of crude oil during discharged

CPA/TCPA	Closest Point of Approach /Time to Closest Point of Approach limit as defined by the observer to give warning when a tracked target or targets will close to within these limits
Crash-stop	An emergency reversal operation of the main engine(s) to avoid a collision
Damage control team	A group of crew members trained for fighting flooding in the vessel
Datum	1. The most probable position of a search target at a given time 2. The plane of reference to which all data as to the depth on charts are referenced.
Derelict	Goods or any other commodity, specifically a vessel abandoned at sea
Destination	Port which a vessel is bound for
Disabled	A vessel damaged or impaired in such a manner as to be incapable of proceeding on its voyage
Disembark (to)	To go from a vessel
Distress alert (GMDSS)	A radio signal from a distressed vessel automatically directed to an MRCC giving position, identification, course and speed of the vessel as well as the nature of distress
Distress/ Urgency	here: The verbal exchange of information on
traffic	radio from ship to shore and/or ship to ship/ air craft about a distress / urgency situation as defined in the relevant ITU Radio Regulations
Draught = Draft [6]	The depth of water which a vessel draws

---

6) 고대 게르만어의 '끌다'를 뜻하는 *dragan*(현대 독일어 tragen)에서 기원한 말인데, 이 말이 고대 노르만어에서는 drahtr나 dráttr로 사용되었고, 중세 네덜란드어에서는 dragt, 고대 고지 게르만 어에서는 traht(현대 독일어의 tracht) 등으로 사용되다가 영어에 유입된 말이다. 결국 draught는 '배가 끌어들인(마신) 물의 양'이란 뜻에서 기원한 말인 셈이다. 영어 draw는 다양한 용법으로 사용되고 있고, 그 명사형인 draught도 마찬가지다.

Dragging (of anchor)	Moving of an anchor over the sea bottom involuntarily because it is no longer preventing the movement of the vessel = **走錨**
Dredging (of anchor)	Moving of an anchor over the sea bottom to control the movement of the vessel = **引錨**
Drifting	Floating, caused by winds and current with a determinable direction
Drop back (to)	To increase the distance to the vessel ahead by reducing one's own speed
DSC	Digital Selective Calling (in the GMDSS system)
Embark (to)	To go aboard a vessel
EPIRB	Emergency Position Indicating Radio Beacon
Escape route	A clearly marked way in the vessel which has to be followed in case of an emergency
Escort	Attending a vessel, to be available in case of need, e.g. ice-breaker, tug, etc..
ETA	Estimated Time of Arrival
ETD	Estimated Time of Departure
Fire patrol	A crew member of the watch going around the vessel at certain intervals so that an outbreak of fire may be promptly detected; mandatory in vessels carrying more than 36 passengers
Flooding	Major flow of seawater into the vessel
Fire monitor	Fixed foam/powder/water cannon shooting fire extinguishing agents on tank, deck, manifold etc.
Foul (of anchor)	Anchor has its own cable twisted around it or has fouled an obstruction
Foul (of propeller)	A line, wire, net, etc., is wound round the propeller

Full speed	Highest possible speed of a vessel
Fume	Often harmful gas produced by fires, chemicals, fuel, etc.
General emergency alarm	A sound signal of seven short blasts and one prolonged blast given with the vessel´s sound system
GMDSS	Global Maritime Distress and Safety System
(D) GPS	(Differential) Global (satellite) Positioning System
Hampered vessel	A vessel restricted by her ability to manoeuver by the nature of her work or her deep draft
Hatchrails	Ropes supported by stanchions around an open hatch to prevent persons from falling into a hold
Heading	The horizontal direction the vessel's bows at a given moment measured in degrees clockwise from north
Hoist	here: A cable used by helicopters for lifting or lowering persons in a pick-up operation
Icing	Coating of ice on an object, e.g. the mast or superstructure of a vessel
IMO-Class	Group of dangerous or hazardous goods, harmful substances or marine pollutants in sea transport as classified in the International Maritime Dangerous Goods Code (IMDG Code)
Inert (to)	To reduce the oxygen in an oil tank by inert gas to avoid an explosive atmosphere
Initial course	Course directed by the OSC or other authorized person to be steered at the beginning of a search
Inoperative	Not functioning
Jettison (to) (of cargo)	Throwing overboard of goods in order to lighten the vessel or improve its stability in case of an emergency

Launch (to)	To lower, e.g. lifeboats to the water
Leaking	Escape of liquids such as water, oil, etc., out of pipes, boilers, tanks, etc., or a minor inflow of seawater into the vessel due to damage to the hull
Leeward	The general direction to which the wind blows; opposite of windward = 바람이 불어가는 쪽
Leeway	The angular effect on the vessel's course caused by the prevailing wind = 풍압차
Let go (to)	To set free, let loose, or cast off (of anchors, lines, etc.)
Lifeboat station	Place assigned to crew and passengers where they must gather before being ordered into the lifeboats
List	here: Inclination of the vessel to port side or starboard side
Located	In navigational warnings: Position of object confirmed
Make water (to)	Seawater flowing into the vessel due to hull damage, or hatches awash and not properly closed
MMSI	Maritime Mobile Service Identity number
Moor (to)	To secure a vessel in a particular place by means of wires or ropes made fast to the shore, to anchors, or to anchored mooring buoys, or to ride with both anchors down
MRCC	Maritime Rescue Co-ordination Centre: Land-based authority responsible for promoting efficient organization of maritime search and rescue and for co-ordinating the conduct of search and rescue operations within a search and rescue region

Muster (to)	To assemble crew, passengers or both in a special place for purposes of checking
Muster list	List of crew, passengers and all on board and their functions in a distress or drill
Not under command	(abbr. NUC) A vessel which through exceptional circumstances is unable to manoeuver as required by the COLREGs
Obstruction	An object such as a wreck, net, etc., which blocks a fairway, route, etc.
Off air	When the transmissions of a radio station etc., have broken down, been switched off or suspended
Off station (of buoys)	Not in charted position
Oil clearance	Oil skimming from the surface of the water
Operational	Ready for immediate use
Ordnance exercise	Naval firing practice
OSC	On-Scene Co-ordinator: A person designed to co-ordinate search and rescue operations within a specified area
Overflow	Accidental escape of oil from a tank which is full because pumping was not stopped in time
Polluter	A vessel emitting harmful substances into the air or spilling oil into the sea
Preventers	Ropes or wires attached to derricks to prevent them from swinging during cargo handling operations
Proceed (to)	To sail or head for a certain position or to continue with the voyage

PA-system	Public address system: Loudspeakers in the vessel's cabins, mess rooms, etc., and on deck through which important information can be broadcast from a central point, mostly from the navigation bridge
Recover (to)	Here: To pick up shipwrecked persons
Refloat (to)	To pull a vessel off after grounding; to set afloat again
Rendezvous	An appointment between vessels normally made on radio to meet in a certain area or position
Reported	in navigational warnings: Position of object unconfirmed
Restricted area	A deck, space, area, etc., in vessels, where for safety reasons, entry is only permitted for authorized crew members
Resume (to)	here: To re-start a voyage, service or search
Retreat signal	Sound, visual or other signal to a team ordering it to return to its base
Rig move	The movement of an oil rig, drilling platform, etc., from one position to another
Roll call	The act of checking who of the passengers and crew members are present, e.g. at assembly stations, by reading aloud a list of their names
Safe speed	That speed of a vessel allowing the maximum possible time for effective action to be taken to avoid a collision and to be stopped within an appropriate distance
Safety load	The maximum permissible load of a deck, etc.
Safe working pressure	The maximum permissible pressure in cargo hoses
SAR	Search and Rescue

Scene	The area or location where the event, e.g. an accident has happened
Search pattern	A pattern according to which vessels and/or aircraft may conduct a coordinated search (the IMO SAR offers seven search patterns)
Search speed	The speed of searching vessels directed by the OSC
Seamark	An elevated object on land or sea serving as a guide .....
Segregation(of goods)	Separation of goods which for different reasons must not be stowed together
Shackle	Standard length (15 fathoms) of an anchor cable
Shifting cargo	Transverse movement of cargo, especially bulk, caused by rolling or a heavy list
Slings	Ropes, nets, and any other means for handling general cargoes
Speed of advance	The speed at which a storm centre moves
Spill (to)	The accidental escape of oil, etc., from a vessel, container, etc., into the sea
Spill control gear	Special equipment for fighting accidental oil spills at early stages
Spreader	here: Step of a pilot ladder which prevents the ladder from twisting
Stand by (to)	To be in readiness or prepared to execute an order; to be readily available
Stand clear (to)	here: To keep a boat away from the vessel
Standing orders	Orders of the Master to the officer of the watch which s/he must comply with
Stand on (to)	To maintain course and speed

Station	The allotted place or the duties of each person on board
Stripping	Draining tanks of the remaining cargo, water, etc.
Survivor	A person who continues to live in spite of being in an extremely dangerous situation, e.g. a shipping disaster.
Take off (to)	A helicopter lifts off from a vessel's deck
Target	The echo generated e.g. by a vessel on a radar screen
Tension winch	A winch which applies tension to mooring lines to keep them tight
TEU	Twenty Foot Equivalent Unit (standard container dimension)
Track	The path followed, or to be followed, between one position and another
Transit	here: The passage of a vessel through a canal, fairway, etc.
Transit speed	Speed of a vessel required for the passage through a canal, fairway, etc.
Transshipment (of cargo)	here: The transfer of goods from one vessel to another outside harbours
Underway	A vessel which is not at anchor, or made fast to the shore, or aground
Union purchase	A common method of cargo handling by combining two derricks, one of which is fixed over the quay, the other over the hatchway
Unlit	When the light characteristics of a buoy or a lighthouse are inoperative
UTC	Universal Time Co-ordinated (ex GMT)

Variable **(of winds)**	When a wind is permanently changing the direction from which it blows
Veering **(of winds)**	Shifting of wind direction in a manner, in time; opposite of backing = 방향을 바꾸다. 풀어주다
Veer out (to)(of anchors)	To let out a greater length of cable
VHF	Very High Frequency (30 - 300 MHz)
Walk out (to) (of anchors)	To lower the anchor until it is clear of the hawse pipe and ready for dropping
Walk back	To reverse the action of a windlass to ease the cable of anchor
Way point	A position a vessel has to pass or at which she has to alter course according to her voyage plan
Windward	The general direction from which the wind blows; opposite of leeward
Wreck	A vessel which has been destroyed or sunk or abandoned at sea

2   VTS special terms

Fairway	Navigable part of a waterway
Fairway speed	Mandatory speed in a fairway
ITZ	Inshore Traffic Zone (of a TSS): A routing measure comprising a designated area between the landward boundary of a TSS and the adjacent coast
manoeuvering speed	A vessel's reduced rate of speed in restricted waters such as fairways or harbours
Receiving point	A mark or place at which a vessel comes under obligatory entry, transit, or escort procedure
Reference line	A fictive line displayed on the radar screens in VTS Centres and/or electronic sea-charts separating the fairway for inbound and outbound vessels so that they can safely pass each other
Reporting point	A mark or position at which a vessel is required to report to the local VTS-Station to establish her position
Separation zone / line	A zone or line separating the traffic lanes in which vessels are proceeding in opposite or nearly opposite directions; or separating a traffic lane from the adjacent sea area; or separating traffic lanes designated for particular classes of vessels proceeding in the same direction
Traffic clearance	VTS authorization for a vessel to proceed under conditions specified
Traffic lane	An area within defined limits in which one-way traffic is established
TSS	Traffic Separation Scheme: A routing measure aimed at the separation of opposing streams of traffic by appropriate means and by the establishment of traffic lanes

VTS	Vessel Traffic Services: Services, designed to improve safety of navigation and efficiency of vessel traffic and to protect the environment
VTS-area	Area controlled by a VTS-Centre or VTS-Station

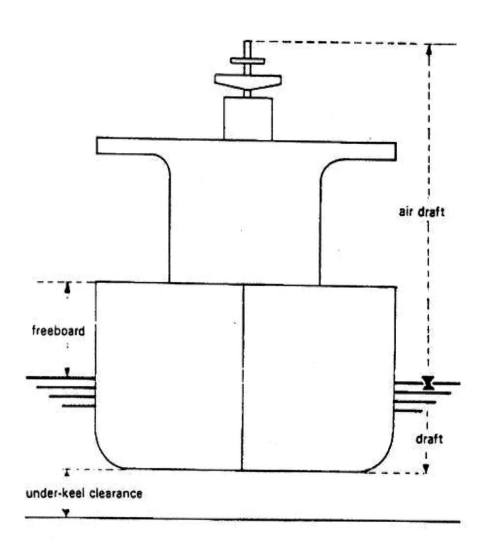

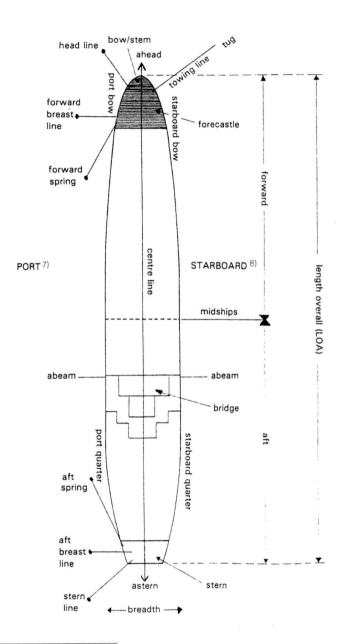

7) **port의 어원** : 라틴어 *portare*(옮기다)에서 porta(문)과 portus(항)이 분화되었는데, 라틴어 *portus*가 영어 port의 어원이다. 고대 로마에서는 새롭게 도시를 계획할 경우 주변에 성벽을 만들기 위해 삽으로 예정선을 파두었는데, 그 예정선을 발로 넘는 것은 완공될 성벽이 적에게 침범되는 흉조라고 하여 엄금하였다. 따라서 몇 개의 성문을 만들 곳은 예정선을 중단할 필요가 있었고, 그 장소에서는 사람들은 삽을 어깨로 들어서 옮겼다. 이와 같은 유래에서 porta(문)과 portus(항)이 portare에서 유래된 것이다. 해사용어 port는 '항'이라는 뜻 외에 선박의 '좌현'을 뜻하는 낱말로 자주 사용된다. 원래 영국에서는 좌현을 larboard라고 하고, 우현을 starboard라고 하였으나, larboard와

starboard가 혼동하기 쉬워 종종 사고를 유발했기 때문에 larboard를 port로 고쳐 부르게 되었다는 것은 잘 알려진 사실이다. larboard는 중앙타가 도입되기 이전 유럽의 선박들은 현측 타(side rudder)를 사용했고, 대체로 오른쪽에 현측 타를 장착하는 게 보통이었기 때문에 항구에 배를 댈 때는 현측 타의 방해를 받지 않는 좌현 쪽으로 계류하는 게 보통이었다. 따라서 배의 좌현은 '짐을 싣는 현'이라는 듯으로 ladde-borde라고 썼던 것이 larboard가 되었다. 그렇다면 larboard가 어느 시점에서 port로 대체되었을까? 사와 센페이는 "영국에서는 1844년 11월 22일 해군 명령, 미국에서는 1년 3개월 후인 1846년 2월 18일 해군의 포고에 의한 것으로 볼 수 있다"고 밝혔다.

8) **starboard의 어원** : 원게르만어 steuro(a steering)에서 기원한 *steor*(키, 타) + *board*(뱃전)이 결합하여 '조타현'(steer-board, side on which a vessel was steered)이라는 의미로 고대영어에서는 steorbord로 사용되었다. 초창기 게르만인들의 배는 오른쪽에서 노(paddle)를 저었기 때문에 '노를 젓는 뱃전'이라는 의미로 steorbord라고 했는데, 이것이 영어에 도입되면서 어형이 변화되어 오늘날 starboard가 된 것이다. 프랑스어 tribord, 이탈리아어 stribordo, 스페인어 estribor, 독일어 Steuerbord, 네덜란드어 stuurboord 등이 모두 게르만어를 차용한 말이다. 그리스와 로마의 갤리선, 바이킹의 배 등은 모두 노를 젓는 배였으므로 별도의 키가 필요없었다. 따라서 유럽의 경우 선미의 중앙에 타를 설치하게 된 것은 12세기 독일 한자동맹의 cog선에 이르러서였다.

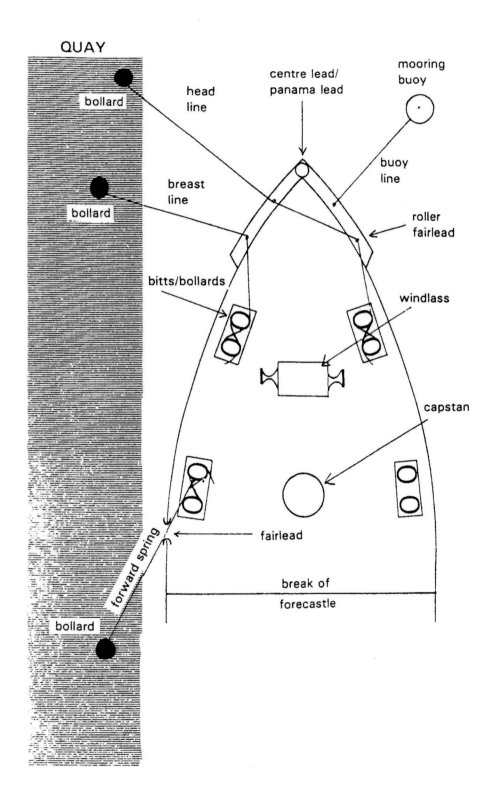

● bitt : 계선주(繫船柱)

어원이 불분명하지만 대체로 저지 게르만어에서 유래한 것으로 보인다. 고대 독일어에서 나무 말뚝(wooden peg)의 뜻으로 bit나, 고대 노르만어에서 대들보(crossbeam)의 뜻으로 biti가 사용되었다.

● bollard : 계선주(繫船柱)

배를 안벽에 매어 두는 기둥을 *bollard*라고 부르는데, 이것은 *bole*(나무줄기) + ~*ard*(~하는 사람 또는 ~하는 물건)의 합성어로 볼 수 있다

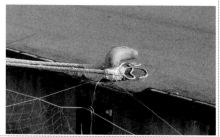

● capstan : 권양기(捲揚機)

'쥐다', '잡다'를 뜻하는 라틴어 capere(영어 capture의 어원)의 현재분사형 *capitstrans*에서 기원한 낱말로, capstan의 어원을 고려하면, 옛 선원들이 맨손으로 닻줄을 당겨 끌어 올릴 때 가장 중요한 것은 닻줄이 다시 끌려 내려가지 않게 꽉 잡아두는 것이었음을 알 수 있다.

● windlass : 양묘기(揚錨機)

'감다'를 뜻하는 고대 노르만어 'vinda'에서 유래한 'vindass'와 '기둥'이나 '들보'를 뜻하는 'ass'가 결합해 만들어진 단어가 13세기 말 경 'wyndase'로 사용되다가 1400년 경 실린더 둘레에 로프를 감아 돌려 무거운 것을 들어올리는 기계를 뜻하는 의미로 사용되었다. 결국 capstan과 windlass는 라틴어 어원과 노르만어 어원이라는 것만 다를 뿐 그 원래 뜻은 같았다.

III Standard Maritime Communication Practice

1. INTRODUCTION OF MARITIME COMMUNICATIONS[9]

1.1 General

Vessels on long voyages are often away from land for weeks or months at a time. Even on short voyages, a sailor on a boat is isolated from the land, and it is often difficult to know what is happening only a short distance away. Unless one is close enough to simply yell to people on shore or aboard other vessels, questions must often go unanswered until one returns home. It was natural, then, that early mariners would embrace technologies that allowed them to communicate across distances.

1.1.1 Written messages

One of the oldest methods of remote communication still exists today. One writes a message on a piece of paper and has it delivered to the recipient. For the sailor at sea, this meant receiving letters and important messages at ports where the vessel stopped or from friendly vessels encountered along the way. In some cases, it could take months or even years for a message to reach the addressee.

An even slower and less reliable way to deliver a written note was to seal it inside an empty bottle and throw it overboard, letting wind and current carry it where they would. With time and luck, some person might actually find and read the note.

---

9) Note: The rest of the text following in this chapter has been adapted from Boris Pritchard, *Maritime communications and IMO SMCP 2001* (Draft version), University of Rijeka, Croatia, 2003.

1.1.2 Flags, semaphores, and other systems

For centuries written correspondence remained the most reliable way to get messages across long distances. However, there were much faster ways for vessels to send simple messages while within sight of the shore or other vessels. Through the use of signal flags and semaphore, a message could be sent to anyone who could see it and understand it. Since these messages were visible to everyone nearby, elaborate codes were developed to identify the sender and recipient and to hide the meaning of the message. When Samuel F. B. Morse developed one of the first practical telegraph systems in 1837, he also designed a code for it in which different combinations of dots and dashes represented letters of the alphabet. Although the telegraph, which required a continuous wire linking the sender and receiver, was useless to mariners, Morse Code was very useful: The heliograph was a bright lamp with a shutter that could be opened and closed to produce a sequence of long and short flashes corresponding to Morse's dots and dashes.

1.1.3 Radio

While early sailors relied only upon written messages, signal flags, semaphores, and a few other signaling techniques to communicate, the twentieth century brought major change to communication. In 1901 an Italian inventor named Marchese Guglielmo Marconi transmitted a radio signal across the Atlantic Ocean, and by 1910 the United States had passed a law requiring its passenger ships to have radio equipment on board. Radio made it possible, for the first time, for a vessel out of sight of land or other vessels to keep in touch with the rest of the world. Radio did not immediately eliminate the need for more traditional signaling systems, however, and many of them, including semaphore and heliograph, were in active use through World War II. Even today, signal flags are carried aboard most large vessels and many smaller ones. Still, radio had a profound impact on communication throughout the world, and particularly on the way sailors communicate.

1.1.4 VHF

There are two basic kinds of radios found aboard ocean-going vessels. Marine VHF (very high frequency) radios require an uninterrupted line of sight between antennas. This limits their range, and they are usually used to communicate over distances of less than about 20-30 nautical miles. Most marine radio traffic occurs over VHF radio, since skippers are naturally most concerned about vessels, port facilities, and hazards in their immediate vicinity.

1.1.5 SSB

To communicate over very long distances, especially while a vessel is at sea, many pleasure craft and virtually all commercial and military vessels are equipped with Marine SSB(single side-band) radio. SSB has a much greater range than VHF because it does not require a line of sight between stations. Its signal "bounces" in the earth's atmosphere, enabling it to reach around the planet's curved surface for thousands of miles. Transmitting on SSB requires a great deal of electricity compared to VHF, however, since its signal must be strong enough to travel over great distances through a lot of atmosphere.

1.1.6 Satellite communication

Satellite communication is a relatively new alternative for long-distance communication. It features many advantages over conventional point-to-point radio. Instead of transmitting an analog signal directly from the vessel to a shore station, a digital signal is transmitted upward to a satellite. The satellite then relays the signal to another satellite or to a receiver elsewhere on the surface of the earth.

Satellite communication is private. When you use conventional SSB or VHF, everybody with a receiver in range can monitor your conversation. Signals transmitted for satellite communication, however, are highly directional, making them much more difficult for the casual eavesdropper to pick up. In the case of digital signals, data can be encrypted, making it extremely secure against even a determined spy. Satellite communication allows direct access to the global communication infrastructure (telephone and computer networks). SSB or VHF, on the other hand, both require an intermediary--such as a ship-to-shore operator-- to make the appropriate connections ashore.

Satellite communication is not greatly affected by atmospheric or meteorological conditions. The signal does not have to bounce since it only needs to reach an overhead satellite, which is always within line-of-sight. Because the signal is being transmitted primarily upward, it passes through a relatively thin layer of the Earth's atmosphere. SSB and VHF transmissions, however, must push their way through a great quantity of distortion-producing atmosphere as they travel across the surface of the Earth.

1.1.7 Geosynchronous satellites

Most communications satellites are in geosynchronous, or geostationary, orbits. This means that each satellite is at an altitude (22,300 miles or so) such that its speed around the earth matches the earth's rotation. Both the satellite and the surface of the Earth are rotating around the Earth's axis, but since they are rotating at the same rate, the satellite appears to stay in one place over the Equator. This simplifies signal transmission since once an antenna on the ground is directed toward the satellite, it does not have to be readjusted. The dish antennas used to receive satellite television are directed toward geosynchronous satellites. A vessel at sea, however, does not stay in one place. Even if it did, though, it would tend to provide an insufficiently stable surface for precise antenna alignment.

1.1.8 InMarSat system

Inmarsat, or International Maritime Satellite, is an international partnership of government and private entities representing 75 countries, Headquartered in London, its charter is to provide mobile satellite communication services to the world. InMarSat was established in 1979 and began providing services in 1982. Currently, InMarSat uses four of its own satellites and leases maritime communication capacity on several other satellites. All of the units in the InMarSat system are in geosynchronous orbits.

1.2 Channel / Frequency Assignments

The frequencies used in marine radiotelephone communication are established for use by specific services in specific locations. These frequencies should only be used for the type of communication for which they were intended.

1.2.1 International Distress, Calling and Answering Frequencies

These frequencies are set aside for the primary use of distress, urgency and safety communications. They may also be used to initiate a call to other stations or to receive their replies, in which case a mutually satisfactory working channel can be determined. Channel 16 (156.800 MHz) on VHF has been designated for this purpose.

Note: A working channel is a channel other than a pre-designated channel that is used for the passage of information or messages from one station to another.

You should never send messages or information an the calling channel. This channel is used for contact only. When it is known that a station you want to communicate with is operating on a working frequency, it is not necessary to employ the calling frequency. It is permissible to wait until the communication terminates and then call the station with which you wish to communicate on the working frequency.

1.2.2 Watchkeeping

When at sea or in port, ships fitted with radiotelephone equipment should keep watch on the frequency 156.800 Mhz. (Channel 16 VHF).

When at sea, ships required by law to be fitted with VHF radiotelephone equipment (compulsorily fitted) must keep a continuous watch on the frequency 156.800Mhz. (Channel 16 VHF) or other frequencies specifically designated on their licences, except when actually engaged in conducting communications on their working frequencies.

For compulsorily fitted vessels, the very high frequency (VHF) regulations state that watchkeeping on the VHF band must begin at least 15 minutes before the vessel leaves its dock or place of mooring. The regulations also state that this watch on Channel 16 (156.800 MHz.) shall not be terminated until the vessel is securely anchored or moored. There are precautions which must be observed when using radiotelephone equipment while a vessel is in port or navigating near coast stations. The regulations governing the use of the transceivers in and around ports and coast stations state that the VHF transceiver will be used in the 1-watt position.

For tanker fleets, it is required to turn-off MF/HF while in port.

1.3 Radio Logs

1.3.1 General

All compulsorily fitted radio stations using maritime mobile frequencies are required to keep a radio log. The activities of the station, as well as the nature of messages and signals transmitted, received or intercepted by the station, are to be recorded in chronological order. The log must be located at the main operating position of the station during the time the ship is on a voyage. The log is to be kept by the operator maintaining the listening watch, in accordance with the Radio Regulations.

A radio log must contain entries recording the following particulars:

.1 the name, port of registration and official registration or license

.2 number of the vessel (or IMO number)

.3 the gross tonnage of the vessel

.4 the frequency or frequencies guarded

.5 the time, whether:

① the local time of the area in which the vessel is operating, or

② the Co-ordinated Universal Time (UTC) when the vessel is engaged in an international voyage, and

.6 the time and reasons for any radio communication interruption.

1.3.2 VHF Radiotelephone Installations

In conjunction with the general information outlined above, ship stations using equipment operating in the maritime mobile VHF band (156.0 MHz - 162.5 MHz) must record the following:

.1 the name(s) of the radio operator(s) on watch, as well as the times of going on and off watch,

.2 a detailed summary of all communications transmitted, received or intercepted relating to distress, urgency or safety traffic, recorded in chronological order,

.3 brief summaries of communications exchanged with other stations with frequency used for reception and transmission,

.4 the time of, and reason for, any discontinuance of the listening watch on frequency 156.800 MHz - Channel 16, and

.5 the times of departure from and arrival at port.

Note:

Watch on Channel 16 (156.8 MHz) can be interrupted by ships in a Vessel Traffic Service(VTS) Zone when they are required to use a channel other than 16 for vessel traffic management purposes. This is because a continuous watch on Channel 16 is maintained for ships by the traffic centre, or by a coast station that is able to establish contact with the traffic centre without delay.

1.4 Frequencies

1.4.1 External communications - Intership Frequencies

A number of frequencies have been set aside specifically for communications between ships. Some of these intership frequencies have been designated as safety frequencies to be used when important messages are to be passed between ships (for example, safety messages).

1.4.2 Public Correspondence Frequencies

Coast Guard or coast radio stations are located at various points along the coasts and the coastal regions of any maritime state. They provide a safety service, including broadcasts of meteorological forecasts and aids to navigation information, as well as facilities for handling messages or telephone conversations between ships and shore. The ship-to-shore frequencies that have been set aside for communicating with coast stations are called public correspondence frequencies.

1.4.3 Vessel Traffic Services Frequencies

In order to promote navigational safety, the protection of the environment and the safe movement of marine traffic, Vessel Traffic Services(VTS) areas have been established throughout the busy waterways & coastal waters. Communications within these areas are conducted on dedicated frequencies. (e.g. Busan VTS Ch.12, Busan New port Ch.10)

1.4.4 Broadcast Frequencies

One of the many tasks of the Coast Guard Agency is to pass information to vessels in the form of notices of danger to navigation or the marine weather forecast. These broadcasts are usually transmitted on dedicated frequencies of VHF (Ch.24) and SSB.

1.4.5 Emergency Frequencies

.1 Distress:
156.800 MHz (Channel 16) Voice
156.525 MHz (Channel 70) Digital Selective Calling (DSC)

.2 Emergency Position Indicating Radio Beacons (EPIRBs):
156-800 MHz (Marine)

1.5 Voice Radio-communications

1.5.1 Superfluous Communications and Interference

.1 Unnecessary Transmissions

Communications should be restricted to those necessary for the safe and expeditious movement of vessels. Unnecessary transmissions are not permitted. Profane and obscene language is strictly prohibited.

.2 False Distress Transmissions

False distress signals are strictly prohibited. Penalty:

Any person who knowingly transmits or causes to be transmitted any false or fraudulent distress signal, call or message is guilty of an offence and is liable, on summary conviction, to a penalty or to imprisonment, or to both.

.3 Interference

All radio stations shall be installed and operated so as not to interfere with or interrupt the working of another radio station.

The only situation under which you may interrupt or interfere with the normal working of another station is when you are required to transmit a higher priority call or message (for example, distress, urgency or safety calls or messages).

1.5.2 Communications Priorities

The order of priority for radiocommunications:

.1 distress communications,   MAYDAY

.2 urgency communications,   PAN-PAN

.3 safety communications,   SECURITE

.4 communications relative to the navigation, movement and needs of aircraft engaged in search and rescue operations,

.5 messages containing exclusively meteorological (weather) observations destined to an official meteorological office,

.6 communications related to the application of the United Nations Charter,

.7 service messages relative to the working of the radiocommunications service or to messages that have been previously transmitted,

.8 all other communications.

1.6 General VHF Radio Conduct

You should be aware that all bridge conversations could be used as *evidence for inappropriate ship operation* including the *Maritime English performance* involved in case of an incident, accident, distress, etc.

Voyage Data Recording

VHF communications relating to the ship operations should be recorded. One or more microphones positioned on the bridge should be placed so that conversations at or near the conning station, radar displays, chart tables etc., are adequately recorded. As far as practicable the positioning of microphones should also capture intercom, public address systems and audible alarms on the bridge. The time for which all stored data items are retained should be at least 12 hours. Data items which are older than this may be overwritten with new data.

1.6.1 Microphone Techniques

The efficient use of radiotelephone depends to a large extent on the operator's method of speaking. Special care is necessary in their pronunciation. Special care is also required in handling the microphone. Do not hold the microphone too close to your mouth because it may cause distortion or slurring of words and you may have to repeat your message to be understood. Speak all words plainly and end each word clearly in order to prevent the running together of consecutive words.

☎ MIC 누른 후 1~2초 후 말하기, 버튼에서 손 떼고 듣기

1.6.2 Speed and rhythm of speech

Keep the rate of speech constant, neither too fast nor too slow. Remember that the operator receiving your message may have to write it down. Preserve the rhythm of ordinary conversation. Avoid the introduction of unnecessary sounds such as "ER & UM"(filler words) between words.

1.6.3 VHF Radio 사용원칙

General principles	
1	Do not make unnecessary transmissions.
2	Always follow the prescribed VHF Radio Regulations and procedures.
3	Speak more slowly than in normal conversation, especially when the addressee is writing down your message.
4	Maintain a constant voice level.
5	Pronounce each word clearly and spell it if necessary.
6	Always follow established Maritime English practice, particularly the application of Message Markers and IMO SMCP.
7	Always be concise and unambiguous.
8	Use fixed formats, e.g. MAREP(MAriner REPort) etc., where applicable. *The application of MAREP will especially be dealt with.*

	Before transmitting
1	Make sure that your call is really necessary. *Do not jam VHF channels with trivial communications.*
2	Plan what you want to say before starting, write it down if necessary.
3	Check that the VHF set is switched to the correct VHF channel. *Check working channels of coast stations in the latest ITU(int'l Telecommunication Union) List of Coast Stations.*
4	If you want to call another ship, tell that ship which working channel should be used for the exchange. *It will save problems later if, before you choose a working channel, you make certain that it is not already in use.* *First listen – then speak.*
5	Do not interrupt other stations VHF exchanges. *It can be dangerous to interrupt VHF communication in progress; it is even illegal to interrupt Distress and Urgency traffic.*

6	Do not make unauthorized transmissions.
	It is forbidden to:
	    ·transmit false or misleading signals,
	    ·transmit without identification
	    ·make unnecessary or superfluous transmissions.

2. SMCP General

2.1 Phonetic Alphabet

The words of the International Telecommunication Union (ITU) phonetic alphabet should be learned thoroughly. Whenever isolated letters or groups of letters are pronounced separately, or when communication is difficult, the phonetic alphabet can be easily used.

Call signs are always spoken using the International Phonetic Alphabet, no matter which language is used. Vessels have to identify and be addressed with names and call signs. In exceptional cases, when no misunderstanding is possible, the call sign may be skipped, but this is not covered by the Radio Regulations. However, when a vessel's name is complicating, the call sign is a useful tool to identify the vessel.

When a spelling is necessary, only the following spelling table should be used:

Letter	Code	Letter	Code
A	ALFA	N	NOVEMBER
B	BRAVO	O	OSCAR
C	CHARLIE	P	PAPA
D	DELTA	Q	QUEBEC
E	ECHO	R	ROMEO
F	FOXTROT	S	SIERRA
G	GOLF	T	TANGO
H	HOTEL	U	UNIFORM
I	INDIA	V	VICTOR
J	JULIET	W	WHISKEY
K	KILO	X	X-RAY
L	LIMA	Y	YANKEE
M	MIKE	Z	ZULU

2.1.1 Phonetic Alphabet Practice 1

Name of vessels consisting of more than one word are spelt like this:

MV Yussuf Hassan: "Yankee – Uniform – Sierra – Sierra – Uniform – Foxtrot next word (or second word) Hotel – Alfa – Sierra – Sierra – Alfa – November

Spell the names/ call sings listed in the table below:

No.	Name of the vessel	Call sign	Flag state
1	MV Roland	DWST	G
2	Ferry Brigitte	JOLM	N
3	MT Bernd	GFVX	UK
4	MV Sven II	SKYP	S
5	MV Atanathias Pallikaris	J4BC	GR
6	USS Rambo	KW 39751	US
7	MV Takeshi Maru	JAST	J
8	MV Akademik Kholodilnikov	RM2F	RF
9	Training Sailing Ship Pallada	UDUI	RUS
10	VLCC Al Hadjibarakh	HZAA	SAUD
11	Frigate Nordrhein-Westfalen	DFGZ	G
12	Tender Malibu	VNDG	AUS
13	Passenger Liner Golden Dream	LKPP	ARG
14	Factory Vessel Rybolovitelj	EM7Y	UKR
15	RORO Ferry Panstar Dream	DSFU2	KOR
16	MV Lourdes	AMAT	ESP
17	MV Commandante Rios	CLAV	CUB
18	MT Grzegorz	HFDZ	PL
19	MV Yussuf Hassan	5CAG	MOR
20	Passenger Liner Ruocco	9YZZ	TR
21	Ferry Oeiras	XXDZ	POR
22	ULCC Kharetj	HNAS	IRQ
23	Catamaran Virenque	THAA	F
24	PCC Glovis Cardinal	V7CC2	SING
25	Dredger Deep Hole	A8A2	LIB

No.	Spell the Above Ship's Name in Phonetic Alphabet
1	
2	
3	
4	
5	
6	
7	
8	
9	
10	
11	
12	
13	
14	
15	
16	
17	
18	
19	
20	
21	
22	
23	
24	
25	

2.1.2 Phonetic Alphabet Practice 2

Listen to the following parts of radio messages, write down the names spelt

(※Recording : 1A Rec1)

1	*This is motor vessel* _____ *I spell the name of my vessel:* _____, *next word:* _____. *Motor vessel* _____
2	*This is motor vessel* _____. *I spell the name of my vessel:* _____ *next word:* _____. *Motor vessel* _____
3	*My agent is* _____. *I spell the name of my agent:* _____ *next word:* _____*next word:* _____. _____.
4	*My destination is* _____, *I spell the name of the port:* _____. *I repeat:* _____.
5	*The name of the VTS Centre is* _____. *I spell the name of the VTS Centre:* _____. _____.
6	*The name of the captain is* _____. *I spell the name of the captain:* _____, *second word:* _____ *mistake second word – correction:* _____. _____.
7	*The charted name of the Superbuoy is* _____. *I spell the name of the Superbuoy:* _____, *next word:* _____. *Superbuoy* _____.
8	*The name of the tug is* _____, *call sign* _____. *I spell the name of the tug:* _____, *next word:* _____. *Tug* _____.

9	*The charted name of the reef is* _____ *I spell the name of the reef:* _____, *next word:* _____, *next word :* _____. _____
10	*This is motor vessel* _____, *call sign* _____ *I spell the name of my vessel:* _____, *second word:* _____. *Motor vessel* _____.

2.2 **Numbers** (Spelling of digits and numbers)

A few digits and numbers have a modified pronunciation compared to general English:

Number	Spelling	Pronunciation
0	ZERO	ZEERO
1	ONE	WUN
2	TWO	TOO
3	THREE	TREE
4	FOUR	FOWER
5	FIVE	FIFE
6	SIX	SIX
7	SEVEN	SEVEN
8	EIGHT	AIT
9	NINE	NINER
1000	(one)　THOUSAND	(one) TOUSAND

※ 2.1.2 Answer :　　1. Molodaya Rossiya　　2. Nakamutako Maru

3. Jose El Granjo　　4. Pittasaarii　　　　5. Zonguldak

6. Hassan Beradj　　7. Groote Eylandt　　8. Mighty Hippo

9. Curno Del Toro　　10. Maersko Mindanao

Figure	Spelling as spoken	Pronunciation
9	nine	NINER
18	one-eight	WUN-AIT
35	three-five	TREE-FIFE
217	two-one-seven	TOO-WUN-SEVEN
41,000	four-one-thousand	FOWER-WUN-TOUSAND
41,783	four-one-seven-eight-three	FOWER-WUN-SEVEN-AIT-TREE
410,000	four-one-zero-thousand	FOWER-WUN-ZEERO-TOUSAND
28.02	two-eight decimal zero-two or: two-eight point zero-two	TOO-AIT DECIMAL ZEERO- TOO or: TOO-AIT POINT ZEERO-TOO

All numbers except whole thousands should be transmitted by pronouncing each digit separately. Whole thousands should be transmitted by pronouncing each digit in the number of thousands followed by the word THOUSAND (pronounced /ˈtauznd/).

30 becomes   TREE ZEERO

25 becomes   TOO FIFE

100 becomes   WUN ZEERO ZEERO

6,700 becomes   SIX SEVEN ZEERO ZEERO

11,000 becomes   WUN WUN TOUSAND

38,006 becomes   THEE AIT ZEERO ZEERO SIX

Numbers continuing a decimal point should be transmitted as above, with the decimal point indicated by the word DECIMAL.

156.8 becomes   **WUN FIFE SIX DECIMAL AIT**

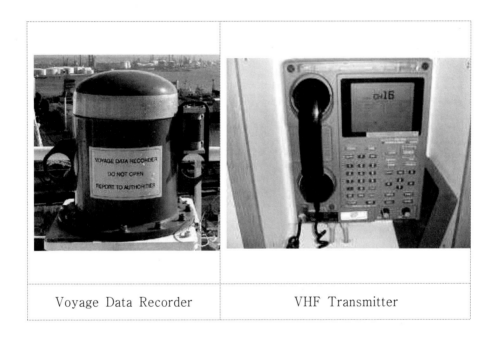

| Voyage Data Recorder | VHF Transmitter |

2.3 Message Marker

In order to especially facilitate shore-to-ship and ship-to-shore communication or when one of the IMO SMCP will not fit the meaning desired, one of the following eight message markers may be used to increase the probability of the purpose of the message being properly understood. It is at the discretion of the shore personnel or the ship's officer whether to use one of the message markers and if so which of them to apply depending on the user's qualified assessment of the situation. If used, the message marker is to be spoken before the message or the corresponding part of the message. The IMO VTS Guidelines recommend that in any message directed to a vessel it should be clear whether the message contains Information, Advice, Warning, or Instruction and IMO SMCP should be used where practicable.:

QUESTION	*QUESTION:* *What is your course?* *What is your position?* *How many tugs are required?* *What is your ETA Fairway Buoy?* *Is buoy Number 1- 4 in correct position?* *What are your intentions?*
ANSWER	*ANSWER:* *My course is 1-3-2 degrees true.* *My position is: NE of Buoy Number 15.* *I require two tugs.* *My ETA Fairway Buoy is: 1-5-4-5 hours local time.* *Negative. Buoy Number 1-4 is not in correct position.*

REQUEST	*REQUEST:*
	Immediate tug assistance.
	Please arrange for the berth on arrival.
	Permission to enter the Fairway.
	Please confirm your DWT.
	Please send a doctor.
INFORMATION	*INFORMATION :*
	Wind backing and increasing.
	The tanker XEROX is next.
	My ETA at Outer Pilot Station is 12:00 hours.
ADVICE (STRONGLY RECOMMENDED, at receiver's option)	*ADVICE:*
	(Advise you) Stand by on channel 6 – 8.
	Steer course: 2-5-3 degrees true.
	Anchor in position: bearing: one-two-five degrees true, from Punta Stella, distance two miles.
INSTRUCTION (SAME AS ORDER, COMMAND OR PROHIBITION)	*INSTRUCTION:*
	You must alter course to starboard.
	Go to berth No. 15.
	Stop your engine immediately.
	Alter course to: new course 1-2-3 true.
	Push on starboard bow.
WARNING	*WARNING:*
	Vessel not under command in position … .
	Obstruction in the fairway.
	Tanker aground in position …
	Gale force winds in area …
	Buoy number: one-five unlit / off position.
	Pilotage services suspended.
INTENTION	*INTENTION:*
	I intend to alter course to starboard and pass astern of you.
	I will reduce speed.
	I will pass astern of you.
	I intend to be underway within two hours.

Other high priority marker words:

DISTRESS   e.g. MAYDAY

URGENCY   e.g. PAN PAN

SAFETY   e.g. SECURITE

2.4 Message Marker Practice

2.4.1 Message Marker Practice 1

It is not always very clear whether INSTRUCTION or ADVICE, WARNING or INFORMATION etc. should be applied. This decision may depend on the speaker's appraisal of the situation given.

No.	Message Marker	Message (SMCP)
1		MV Roberto / SAMK aground in position 2 nm south of buoy bravo.
2		What is local time?
3		Local time is UTC plus two.
4		You must anchor at 09:15 hours local time.
5		Your orders changed.
6		I will stop in present position.
7		Change to VHF Channel 63.
8		MV Emily / IGFR requires two tugs.
9		Passenger liner Atlanta / NFTX not under command

10		Do not arrive after 19:00hours UTC.
11		MT Sarah / G9KK sinking after collision.
12		My position 202degrees, 2.3nm from Red Cliffs.
13		MV Clarissa / FF4T does not agree to be overtaken.
14		Get underway.
15		No, I am not dragging anchor.
16		Danger of icing near Cape Frost
17		The result of search is negative.
18		Report number of persons on board.
19		The maximum permitted draft is 14m.
20		You must stay clear of the fairway.

❀ 2.4.1 Answer

1. warning / information   2. question   3. answer   4. instruction

5. information   6. intention   7. advice   8. request

9. warning / information   10. advice   11. information   12. information

13. warning / information   14. advice   15. answer   16. warning

17. information   18. advice   19. information   20. instruction

2.4.2 Message Marker Practice 2

No.	Message Marker	Message
1		Stop in present position.
2		Advise you steer a new course of 168degrees.
3		Vessel not under command in position to the South of you.
4		Leading light Nora 3unlit.
5		My cargo is 22,000tons of gravel.
6		Say again your position.
7		Wind direction Northwest, force Beaufort 8.
8		Visibility in my position is 300m.
9		Is the depth of water sufficient in the fairway?
10		I will stay in position Ice Bank until 0400 hours UTC.
11		When will the pilot embark?
12		Your berth is not clear until 13:20 local time.
13		I require navigational assistance.
14		Your place in convoy is No. 3(three).
15		Please arrange bunkering before I arrive. (no standard phrase available)
16		Keep clear of VLCC Manolo / FGGT.
17		How was your position obtained?
18		You must anchor clear of fairway.
19		Vessel constrained by her draft in position buoy C2.
20		You must not leave your place in the convoy. (not covered by a standard phrase)

✿ 2.4.2 Answer

1. instruction   2. advice   3. inform./ warn.   4. warning

5. information   6. request   7. information   8. information

9. question   10. intention   11. question   12. information

13. request   14. information   15. request   16. advice

17. question   18. instruction   19. warning   20. instruction

2.5 Date, Time, UTC

2.5.1 Time

The twenty-four hour clock system should be used in expressing time in the Maritime Mobile Service indicating whether UTC, zone time or local time is being used. It should be expressed and transmitted by means of four figures, the first two denoting the hour past midnight and the last two the minutes past the hour. Some examples of time using the twenty-four hour clock system are shown below:

Some Times as Expressed by Radiotelephone

TIME	EXPRESS AS:	
12:45 a.m.	0045	ZERO ZERO FOUR FIVE
12:00 noon	1200	ONE TWO ZERO ZERO
12:45 p.m.	1245	ONE TWO FOUR FIVE
12:00 midnight	0000	ZERO ZERO ZERO ZERO
1:30 a.m.	0130	ZERO ONE THREE ZERO
1:46 p.m.	1345	ONE THREE FOUR FIVE
8:30 p.m.	2030	TWO ZERO THREE ZERO

Co-ordinated Universal Time (UTC)[10] (previous known as Greenwich Mean Time GMT) is normally used in radiocommunications, and the letter Z[11] is an accepted abbreviation for UTC, for example, 0520Z, 2140Z.

---

10) UTC(Coordinated Universal Time)란 1972년 1월 1일부터 세계 공통으로 사용하고 있는 표준시를 말한다. UTC는 '국제도량형국'(International Bureau of Weights and Measures, BIPM)과 '국제 지구자전 좌표국'(International Earth Rotation and Reference Systems Service, IERS)기관이 관리하며, 표준주파수 및 시보(standard frequency and time signal)로 통보하고 있다. UTC의 초신호 간격은 '국제 원자시'(International Atomic Time, TAI), 즉, 국제단위계(SI)의 시간 단위인 초의 정의에 따라 세계 각지에서 운용되는 원자시계로부터의 데이터를 근거로 하므로 국제도량형국이 결정하는 원자시와 정확하게 일치한다.

UTC를 채택할 당시에 미국의 ITU(International Telecommunication Union, 국제전기통신연합)와 프랑스의 IAU(International Astronomical Union, 국제천문연맹)는 서로 각국의 어순에 따라 약어를 쓰고자 했지만, 혼란방지와 모든 언어권에서의 사용, 영어 또는 프랑스어 중 한쪽으로의 편향 방지를 위해 새로운 약어 하나로 통일할 필요성이 존재했다.

UTC는 원래 각각 영어로는 *CUT(Coordinated Universal Time)*와 프랑스어로는 *TUC(Temps Universel Coordonné)*라고 표기한다. 알파벳 'C','U','T'가 공통으로 속한다는 것을 알 수 있다. 또한, 이에 앞서 1925년 1월 1일부터 시간체계를 자정에서 시작하는 것으로 개정한 세계시(UT)를 살펴보면 별의 자오선 통과를 관측한 UT0, 지구 극운동을 고려한 UT1 등의 체계에서 그 형태를 이어 받아 종합적인 결과로 영어의 CUT와 프랑스어의 TUC가 아닌 UTC가 하나의 통일된 표기가 되었음을 추정할 수 있다. 다만, 현재 UTC의 본말을 'Coordinated Universal Time'라고 하는 것은 영어식 표기임을 알 수 있다.(이상 항해학부 2017학번 주성현)

11) 1. 1920년대 이래 GMT 0인 시간대를 'Zone description of zero hours'로 사용.
　　2. NATO 소속 pilot들의 비행지역 code 중 Z = UTC 0인 지역.

Military Time Zones Chart

Zone Letter	Zone Name	Time Offset	Major City
A	Alpha	GMT + 1 Hour	Paris, France
B	Bravo	GMT + 2 Hours	Athens, Greece
C	Charlie	GMT + 3 Hours	Moscow, Russia
D	Delta	GMT + 4 Hours	Kabul, Afghanistan
E	Echo	GMT + 5 Hours	New Delhi, India
F	Foxtrot	GMT + 6 Hours	Dhanka, Bangladesh
G	Golf	GMT + 7 Hours	Bangkok, Thailand
H	Hotel	GMT + 8 Hours	Beijing, China
I	India	GMT + 9 Hours	Tokyo, Japan
J	Julie	Local Time	Local Time Zone
K	Kilo	GMT + 10 Hours	Sidney, Australia
L	Lima	GMT + 11 Hours	Honiara, Solomon Islands
M	Mike	GMT + 12 Hours	Wellington, New Zealand
N	November	GMT - 1 Hour	Azores
O	Oscar	GMT - 2 Hours	Godthab, Greenland
P	Papa	GMT - 3 Hours	Buenos Aires, Argentina
Q	Quebec	GMT - 4 Hours	Halifax, Nova Scotia
R	Romeo	GMT - 5 Hours	New York, NY United States
S	Sierra	GMT - 6 Hours	Dallas, TX United States
T	Tango	GMT - 7 Hours	Denver, CO United States
U	Uniform	GMT - 8 Hours	Los Angeles, CA United States
V	Victor	GMT - 9 Hours	Juneau, AK United States
W	Whiskey	GMT - 10 Hours	Honolulu, HI United States
X	X-Ray	GMT - 11 Hours	Nome, AK United States
Y	Yankee	GMT - 12 Hours	Suva, Fiji
Z	Zulu	GMT (Universal Time)	Greenwich, England

2.5.2 Date & Time

Where the date, as well as the time of day, are required to be shown (as in the radio log or a message preamble), a six (6) figure group should be used. The first two figures indicate the day of the month, the following four figures indicate the time.

> *e.g. 120542 (= 12th day of the current month, time: 05hours 42minutes)*

2.6 Position

2.6.1 Geographical position (latitude and longitude)

Expressed in degrees and minutes (plus decimals of a minute if necessary), north or south of the Equator and east and west of Greenwich. (N, S, E, W)

> *e.g. : GP = 15.25 N, 031.20 W*
> *POSITION: LATITUDE ONE - FIVE DEGREES TWO - FIVE MINUTES NORTH, LONGITUDE ZERO - THREE - ONE DEGREES TWO – ZERO MINUTES WEST*
> *e.g.:　WARNING. Dangerous wreck in position 15 degrees 34 minutes North 061 degrees 29 minutes West.*

2.6.2 Bearing and distance:

True bearings are to be given from an object followed by distance in NM or fractions of a mile. Use the words: BEARING and DISTANCE.

> *e.g.　POSITION: BEARING 0 - 9 - 5 DEGREES TRUE FROM CAPE MARCO, DISTANCE 2 DECIMAL 6 MILES*

Do not say(highly recommended)

POSITION: BEARING 0 - 9 - 5 DEGREES TRUE,

DISTANCE 2 DECIMAL 6 MILES FROM CAPE MARCO

e.g.: *Your position bearing 137 degrees from Big Head lighthouse distance 2.4 nautical miles.*

2.6.3 Reference to a navigation mark:

The order direction.

distance / progress - name of mark should be followed.

Use points of the compass (North, Southeast); useful phrases: NORTH OF, SOUTH OF; PASSING, APPROACHING, BETWEEN, NEAR, LEAVING:

> *e.g. POSITION: SOUTHWEST OF KALIFRONT POINT*

> *e.g. APPROACHING BUOY NUMBER: BRAVO 1 - 2*

2.7 Bearings

Use the 360 degrees notation from true north (except in the case of relative bearings).

Bearings may be taken either for a ship or a navigational mark:

> *e.g. PILOT BOAT BEARING 2 - 1 - 5 DEGREES FROM YOU*

Relative bearings: bearings relative to the vessel's head or bow (starboard or port bow): Relative bearings can be expressed in degrees relative to the vessel's head. More frequently this is in relation to the port or starboard bow.

> *e.g. Buoy 030 degrees on your port bow.*

2.8 Courses, distances, speed

2.8.1 Courses

Courses are to be expressed in 360 degrees notation from true north. State whether the course is TO or FROM a mark.

2.8.2 Distances

Distances are expressed in nautical miles or cables (tenths of a mile), and less frequently in kilometres or metres. The unit of measurement should always be stated.

⚘ 1 NM = 1.852km, 1 cable = 185.2m, LM = 1.609km

2.8.3 Speed

Speed must be expressed in knots (i.e. nautical miles per hour). Speed is normally understood as speed through the water but ground speed (over the ground) may be indicated if necessary.

2.9 Ambiguous words

Some words in English have meanings depending on the context in which they appear. Misunderstandings frequently occur, especially in VTS communications, and have produced accidents. Such words are:

The conditionals "may", "might", "should" and "could"

MAY

Do not say: "May I enter the fairway?"

Say: "QUESTION. Do I have permission to enter the fairway?"

Do not say: "You may enter the fairway."

Say: "ANSWER. You have permission to enter the fairway."

Do not say: "May I leave the berth?"
Say: "QUESTION: Is it permitted to leave the berth?"

Do not say: "You may enter the fairway."
Say: "ANSWER: It is permitted to enter the fairway."

MIGHT:

Do not say :   "I might drop the anchor
Say: "INTENTION : I will drop the anchor."

Do not say: "I might enter the fairway."
Say: "INTENTION. I will enter the fairway."

SHOULD:

Do not say: "You should anchor east of buoy D 5."
Say: "ADVICE. Anchor east of buoy D 5."

Do not say: "You should anchor in anchorage B 3."
Say: "ADVICE. Anchor in anchorage B 3."

COULD:

Do not say: "You could be running into danger."
Say: "WARNING: You are running into danger."

CAN:

The word "can" describes either the possibility or the capability of doing something. In the IMO SMCP, the situations where phrases using the word "can" appear make it clear whether a possibility is referred to. In an ambiguous context, however, say, for example:

e.g. 1:

Say: "QUESTION. Do I have permission to use the shallow draft fairway at this time?"

Do not say: "~~Can I use~~ the shallow draft fairway at this time?"

if you are asking for a permission. (The same applies to the word "may").

e.g. 2:

Do not say: Can I use the eastern port approach?

Say: Is it permitted to use the eastern port approach?

NOT:

Do not say: "I ~~don't~~ understand."

Say: "I do NOT understand."

e.g. : won't =≫ will not,   can't =≫ can not

2.10 Standard organizational phrases:

When it is advisable to remain on a VHF Channel, say:
"Stand by on VHF Channel ... ."

When it is accepted to remain on the VHF channel indicated, say:
"Standing by on VHF Channel ... ."

When it is advisable to change to another VHF Channel, say:
"Advise (you) change to VHF Channel ... ."
"Advise(you) try VHF Channel... ."

When the changing of a VHF Channel / frequency is accepted, say:
"Changing to VHF Channel ... / frequency ... ."

2.10.1 Corrections

When a mistake is made in a message, say:
"Mistake ..." followed by the word:
"Correction ... " plus the corrected part of the message.

e.g.:
"My present speed is 14 knots
- Mistake. Correction, my present speed is 1-2, one-two, knots."

2.10.2 Readiness

"I am / I am not ready to receive your message."

2.10.3 Repetition

If any part of the message is considered sufficiently important to safeguard, say:

"Repeat ... "

- followed by the corresponding part of the message.

e.g.

"My draft is 12.6 m.

- repeat - one-two decimal 6 metres."

"Do not overtake - repeat - do not overtake."

When a message is not properly heard, say:

"Say again (please)."

2.10.4 Readability code:

In checking the readability of reception use the phrase:

"How do you read (me)?"

This may be answered as follows:

I read you ...

bad / one	with signal strength one (i.e. barely perceptible)
poor / two	with signal strength two (i.e. weak)
fair / three	with signal strength three (i.e. fairly good)
good / four	with signal strength four (i.e. good)
excellent / five	with signal strength five (i.e. very good)

Sometimes, this may be answered as :

(I can hear you) loud and clear.

3. GENERAL MARITIME RADIOTELEPHONE COMMUNICATION

3.1 The standard procedure for VHF communication

Making Contact – First Call

If your first call is not answered, proceed as follows:
- second call after 2 minutes
- third call after another 2 minutes
- then wait for 3 minutes and repeat the procedure.

Name of station called
>   (max. 3x; when conditions are good: 1x)

+   call sign

this is

name of the calling station
>   (max. 3x; when conditions are good: max: 2x)

+   call sign

change to working channel …

over

After first contact with the station called

Name/call sign of the station called
this is
name / call sign of the station calling
{text of message}
over or   out

Note: Each turn in routine communication has to begin with the procedure given in this box! As a rule, the station having started the communication will finish it with the word "out". Occasionally, the words "over and out" are heard, which means that the sender has nothing more to communicate, but will be standing by in case the other station might respond again – however, this procedure is not covered by Regulations. When the identity of a vessel cannot be mistaken, communicators occasionally happen to skip the call sign in the call, but this is also not covered by Regulations.

3.2 Making a call (Calling)

Before transmitting, listen for a period long enough to ensure that harmful interference to transmissions already in progress is not likely to occur. If such interference seems likely, wait until the transmissions in progress are completed before making your call.

A station having a distress, urgency or safety message to transmit is entitled to interrupt a transmission of lower priority.

In making an initial call you may call:

.1 a single / specific ship or station (whose name and / or call sign you know) or

.2 a station whose name you do not know or when referring to all stations in a sea area.

3.2.1 Single Station Call

When establishing communications with a specific station, transmit the name / call sign of the station being called, followed by the name / call sign of the station making the call, as shown in the following example.

Example 1 : Single station call, name of the ship being called is known:

○ SINGAPORE VTS, SINGAPORE VTS, SINGAPORE VTS
○ THIS IS KOREA ACE, KOREA ACE, DS2FL.
　(CALLING) ON CHANNEL 16
○ OVER

(Singapore VTS, Singapore Port Control)

Example 2 : the name and call sign of the ship/station is known:

○ SEA BASS, SEA BASS, SEA BASS VC2234,
○ THIS IS NEWHAVEN RADIO, NEWHAVEN RADIO,
ON CHANNEL 16
○ OVER

3.2.2 General Call (ALL SHIPS, ALL SHIPS, ALL SHIPS)

If the name of the station / ship is unknown:

When an operator wishes to establish communication with any station within range or in a certain sea area, the call should be made to ALL STATIONS or ALL SHIPS, using the same procedure as a single station call.

Example:

○ ALL SHIPS, ALL SHIPS, ALL SHIPS
or
○ ALL STATIONS, ALL STATIONS, ALL STATIONS IN SEA AREA
OF TOKYO BAY
○ THIS IS YOKOHAMA RADIO, YOKOHAMA RADIO, YOKOHAMA
RADIO
○ OVER

3.3 Responding to initial call

When you hear a call directed to your station, reply as soon as possible. In your response you should :

(a) address the station

(b) identify your own station

(c) finish your turn by saying OVER.

You can advise the calling station to proceed with the message by means of the words GO AHEAD, or, if you are occupied, by saying STAND BY followed by the estimated number of minutes until your reply. Do not ignore the call. This may result in unnecessary calling, which uses up valuable air time in a crowded environment.

Example:

KOREA ACE DS2FL THIS IS SINGAPORE RADIO GO AHEAD OVER	KOREA ACE DS2FL THIS IS SINGAPORE RADIO Stand by (for a while.)

3.3.1 Replying to Calls when Information Is Missing

When you hear a call, but are uncertain the call is intended for your station, do not reply until the call is repeated and understood.

When your station is called but the identity of the calling station is uncertain, you should reply immediately, using the words:

Example:

STATION CALLING, THIS IS KOREA ACE DS2FL SAY AGAIN OVER

3.4 Switching to a Working Channel

Switching to a working channel is normally carried out under the guidance of the Controlling Station (coast station, pilot station, port control, VTS, etc.), which is also responsible for establishing contact on the working channel. It follows immediately after contact has been established on the calling channel 16 or any watchkeeping channel. The phrase recommended by IMO SMCP is:

> SWITCH TO (VHF CHANNEL) ...

Other phrases commonly used are:

> CHANGE TO ...
> GO TO ...

Examples:

Calling Station

> PULA, HR5432.
> THIS IS Busan Newport VTS.
> SWITCH TO (VHF CHANNEL) 1 - 0
> OVER

Responding Station

> Busan Newport VTS,
> THIS IS PULA, HR5432.
> AGREE VHF CHANNEL 1 - 0
> OVER

or

> Busan Newport VTS.
> THIS IS PULA, HR5432.
> AGREE: SWITCHING TO VHF CHANNEL 1 - 0
> OVER

If the suggested channel is not available, use the phrase:

> VHF CHANNEL 83 UNABLE.

and then suggest another channel:

> VHF CHANNELS AVAILABLE: 27
>   or
> VHF CHANNELS AVAILABLE: 17 THROUGH 37

Example:

> ALGECIRAS RADIO.
> THIS IS PULA, HR5432.
> VHF CHANNEL AVAILABLE: 2 – 4.
> OVER

If the VHF channel has not been specified by the Controlling Station, the other station may ask the following:

> QUESTION: WHICH VHF CHANNEL?

3.5 Exchange of Messages

This is the central and most important part of any marine VHF communication or conversation. After establishing contact on the calling channel (16) and switching to and establishing contact on a working channel (indicated by the Controlling Station) the two stations (Calling Station and Responding Station) convey their communicative intention by exchanging their turns in one or more exchanges.

This may be any one or, more usually, a combination of the following:

- asking for information (e.g. on arrival at a port or VTS, strait, etc.)

- answering a question (e.g. on berthing arrangements)

- giving / providing information (e.g. on weather or traffic in a sea area)

- making a request (e.g. request for tugs)

- giving instructions and advice (e.g. where to anchor; keep clear)

- warning (e.g. difficult tow ahead)

- communicating intention (e.g. an intended manoeuver)

- agreeing / disagreeing on a topic, etc. (e.g. on the number of tugs)

In the above cases ITU(Int'l Telecommunication Union) radio regulations and IMO SMCP recommend the use of message markers such as: QUESTION, ANSWER, INFORMATION, INSTRUCTION, ADVICE, REQUEST, INTENTION, WARNING.

In the message stage of the maritime VHF or and other radiotelephone conversation two stations (ship - to - ship, ship - to - shore, shore - to - ship exchanges) ask for or give information, make requests, express intentions, give advice, give instructions, transmit warnings, etc. concerning the various topics, subjects and situations in navigation, navigation safety, manoeuvering, ship handling, avoiding

collisions, environment protection, ship's business, port regulations
such as:

- distress, urgency and safety
- search and rescue
- requesting medical assistance
- meteorological information
- navigational warnings
- environmental protection
- helicopter operations
- ice-breaker operations
- vessel traffic services (VTS)
  - traffic information
  - route information
  - navigational warnings
  - navigational assistance
  - vessel identification (+ position, course)
  - traffic organisation service
    - arrival, berthing and departure
    - pilotage,
    - towage
    - anchoring
    - port (inward/outward) clearance
  - avoiding dangerous situations
  - canal and lock operations, etc.
- cargo operations, etc.

For the phrases to be used in such situations see IMO SMCP,
A1. EXTERNAL COMMUNICATIONS. (Refer to Annex)

3.6 Termination of Communications

To terminate communications, simply conclude your transmission with the command OUT (which means "conversation is ended and no response is expected").

Examples:

```
NEWHAVEN RADIO
THIS IS MARLIN,
UNDERSTOOD
OUT
```

3.7 Corrections and Repetitions

3.7.1 Corrections and Repetitions during Transmission

When an error has been made in transmission, the word CORRECTION should be spoken, the last correct word or phrase repeated and the correct version transmitted.

Examples:

```
AT/IN POSITION SIX, ONE
MISTAKE, CORRECTION SIX, TWO DEGREES ...

PROCEED TO DOCK No. 4
MISTAKE, CORRECTION DOCK No. 2,
ADVISE : ETA .....
```

3.7.2 Repetitions after Completion

Transmissions or items of transmissions should not be repeated unless requested by the receiving operator.

Repetitions should be requested if reception is doubtful.

If the receiving operator desires a repetition of a message, the words SAY AGAIN should be transmitted. If repetition of only a portion of a message is required, the receiving operator should use the following appropriate phraseology:

SAY AGAIN ALL BEFORE ... (first word satisfactorily received),

SAY AGAIN ALL BETWEEN ... (last word correctly received prior to the missing segment) and ... (first word correctly received after the missing segment).

SAY AGAIN ALL AFTER ... (last word satisfactorily received).

Examples:

NEWHAVEN RADIO
THIS IS NORTH WIND VY3844
SAY AGAIN ALL BEFORE "DOCK"
OVER

PRINCE RUPERT COAST GUARD RADIO
THIS IS SEADOG VZI284
SAY AGAIN ALL BETWEEN "PROCEED" AND TIME"
OVER

HONOLULU COAST GUARD RADIO
THIS IS M/V BOUNTY VC3312
SAY AGAIN ALL AFTER "LATITUDE"
OVER

Request for repetition of specific items of a message should be made by speaking the words SAY AGAIN followed by the identification of the message desired.

Examples:

SAY AGAIN OFFICE OF ORIGIN ;

SAY AGAIN POSITION ;

SAY AGAIN TIME ; ETA ;

3.8 Control of Communications

.1 As a general rule, except in cases of priority communications, the control of radio-communications between a coast station and a ship station lies with the coast station (CS = Controlling Station).

.2 In communications between coast stations and ship stations, the ship station shall comply with instructions given by the coast station in all matters relating to the order and time of transmission, to the choice of frequency and to the duration and suspension of work.

.3 In communications between ship stations, normally the station called is the controlling station. If the station is in agreement with the calling station, it shall transmit an indication from that moment onwards that it will listen on the working frequency or channel announced by the calling station.

.4 However, if the station called is not in agreement with the calling station on the working frequency or channel to be used, it shall transmit an indication of the working frequency or channel to be used.

Note: In cases of distress or urgency communications, the control of the communications lies with the station initiating the priority call.

3.9 Unsuccessful Call

When a station called does not reply to a call sent three times at intervals of two minutes, the calling station shall cease and not renew the call until after an interval of three minutes. Before renewing the call, the calling station shall attempt to ascertain that the station being called is not in communication with another station.

3.10 Signal Checks

3.10.1 Procedure for signal check

It is sometimes necessary to verify that your transmitter and receiver are operational. This can be done by :

1. establishing contact with another ship or a coast station on Channel 16, and changing to working channel,

2. establishing contact on the working channel and conducting your tests (examples below), not exceeding 10 seconds for signal checks,

3. using the readability scale listed below when giving the report, remembering that a readability of 3~5 indicates to the receiving station that it is being copied / received / heard 100 percent.

3.10.2 Readability Scale

1 = Bad (unreadable)

2 = Poor (readable now and then)

3 = Fair (readable with great difficulty)

4 = Good (readable with minor difficulty)

5 = Excellent (perfectly readable)

Examples:

Call

```
Singapore VTS
THIS IS PACIFIC HIGH CY2632
ON CHANNEL 16
SIGNAL CHECK 1, 2, 3, 4, 5
HOW DO YOU READ?
OVER
```

Reply

```
PACIFIC HIGH CY2632
THIS IS Sinngapore VTS
I READ YOU EXCELLENT(5)
            ☞ (loud and clear)
OUT
```

4. VHF COMMUNICATIONS with VTS

4.1 Acquiring Data for a Traffic Image

4.1.1 SMCP Phrases for Acquiring data

(Ref.: Annex IMO SMCP, pp.200-201)

Hong Kong VTS acquiring data from MV Korea Ace	SMCP in VHF-communication between VTS and MV Korea Ace—DS2FL; VHF-message begins: "ADDRESS & IDENTIFY"
VTS wishes to know	*Question:*
· name of the vessel and call sign	*1. What is the name of your vessel and call sign?"*
· vessel's course and speed;	*2. What is your present course and speed?*
· vessel's draft;	*3. What is your present maximum draft?*
· where the vessel is going to;	*4. What is your destination?*
· from what port she is coming;	*5. What was your last port of call?*
· what is the next port that she will go to;	*6. What is your next port of call?*
· whether the vessel is proceeding or not;	*7. Are you underway?*
· her ETA at next waypoint;?	*8. What is your ETA at next waypoint?*
· the vessel's full speed to manoeuver;	*9. What is your full manoeuvering speed?*
· what cargo she is carrying;	*10. What is your cargo?*
· whether she has any dangerous goods aboard;	*11. Do you carry any dangerous goods?*
· if she has any defects.	*12.Do you have any deficiencies?*
MV Korea Ace answers:	*Answer:*
· MV Korea Ace DS2FL;	*1. The name of my vessel is Korea Ace-Call sign Delta Sierra 2 Foxtrot Lima;*
· Course: 125 degrees true - speed 14knots;	*2. My present course is 1-2-5 degrees true - my speed is one four knots;*
· Deepest draft 12.5 m	*3. My present maximum draft is 12.5 meters*
· Destination: Hong Kong;	*4. My port of destination is Hong Kong;*
· Last port: Busan;	*5. My last port of call was Busan;*
· Next port: Singapore;	*6. My next port of call is Singapore;*
· Vessel is proceeding;	*7. Yes, I am underway;*
· Next waypoint at 1400 UTC May 26;	*8. My ETA to next waypoint is 1-4-0-0 hours UTC, May 26;*
· Manoeuvering speed 3 knots;	*9. My full manoeuvering speed is 3 knots;*
· Cargo: 3500 metric tons general cargo;	*10. My cargo is 3-5-0-0 tons of general cargo. (I carry 3500)*
· No dangerous goods on board;	*11. No, I do not carry any dangerous cargo*
· SB ballast pump not working.	*12. Yes, I have following deficiency : starboard ballast pump inoperative".*

4.1.2 MV Hyundai Star/HLAN calls Gordana Traffic

Please listen to the recorded VHF communications between MV Hyundai Star (HLAN) and Gordana Traffic (VTS), and write down what you heard. (❀ 9D Rec 3.2)

MV Hyundai Star/HLAN	Gordana Traffic
call Gordana Traffic on VHF Ch 16	call the MV using her call sign you need following details: - the ship's name spelt - want her to switch to VHF Ch 69
☛ _____	☛ _____
- spell ship's name - inform that you will change to VHF Ch 69	ask her - what flag she flies - at what position she is
☛ _____	☛ _____
call back on VHF Ch 69 and answer that - you fly the flag of Korea - your position is 45°03.11' N, 013°24'E	ask what you can do for her
☛ _____	☛ _____
- your destination is Gordana Port - you want to know the berthing instructions	- you want to know her port last called at - you want to know the kind of cargo
☛ _____	☛ _____

- inform that you come from Lisbon, Portugal - report that you carry 3,403 twenty-foot containers - repeat the number of containers	ask whether she has any dangerous goods
☛ _____ _____ _____ _____ _____	☛ _____ _____ _____ _____ _____
respond that you have 8 twenty-foot containers on deck with a total of 2 t of IMO Class 1	- inform that the port does presently not accept IMO Class 1 goods - inform that the MV has got another order - advise Porto Antares as the new destination
☛ _____ _____ _____ _____ _____	☛ _____ _____ _____ _____ _____
repeat the new order and finish the conversation.	
☛ _____ _____ _____	

❀ IMDG(Int'l Maritime Dangerous Goods)

Class 1=explosive 2=gases 3=flammable liquid 4=flammable solid

4.2 Providing Information Service (INS)

4.2.1 SMCP Phrases for Providing INS

(Ref.: Annex IMO SMCP pp. 202~205)

Information about **traffic image and fairways** by Busan Newport VTS.	SMCP in VHF-communication by VTS to all stations. VHF-message begins: "ADDRESS & IDENTIFY"
There is a vessel entering the fairway.	*Information: vessel is entering the fairway.*
MV OOCL Hong Kong is leaving from the terminal. (399.87x58.8x32.5)	*Information: MV OOCL Hong Kong is leaving. (21,413 TEU, ULCV)*
Vessel two cables West of Todo Is. is on her way to sea.	*Information: vessel in posn. two cables West of Todo Is. is outgoing.*
MV Christina is on her way from one berth to another.	*Information: MV Christina is shifting berth.*
Vessel is making a turn to port.	*Information: vessel altering course to port side.*
Vessel in posn. two miles S of LANBY, on course 350° at a speed of 8 knots is not following the traffic regulations.	*Warning: vessel in posn. two miles South of LANBY, course 3-5-0 degrees, speed 8 knots is not complying with traffic regulations.*
Salvage operation are in progress in posn. 34° 55' N / 128° 46' E. Vessels are requested to keep distance.	*Information: salvage operations in progress, position 3-4 degrees 5-5 minutes North, 1-2-8 degrees 4-6 minutes East - wide berth requested.*
There is a vessel two miles W of the entrance that is hampered by a draught of 21 metres.	*Information: vessel two miles West of entrance constrained by a draft of two one meters.*
Route from anchorage to entrance temporarily not to be used.	*Information: route from anchorage to entrance suspended.*
Inshore traffic lane permanently closed for navigation.	*Information: navigation closed in inshore traffic lane.*
Route around dangerous shoal two miles W of Pierhead has been diverted.	*Information: route around hazardous shoal two miles West of Pierhead diverted.*
Dredger Aurora in position 1.2 mile SW of East breakwater is manoeuvering with difficulty. Vessels must keep clear.	*Information: hampered vessel Aurora in posn. one decimal two mile Southwest of East breakwater; wide berth requested.*

Information about **tides** by INCHON VTS.	SMCP in VHF-communication by VTS to all stations. VHF-message begins: "ADDRESS & IDENTIFY"
Prediction: the tide in the S of Palmido Sea area will be 2 metres below datum.	*Tidal prediction: tide of two meters below datum expected in South of Palmido Sea area .*
Tide is getting low.	*Information: tide falling.*
Tide is getting high.	*Information: tide rising.*
Tide is turning.	*Information: tide slack.*
Tide is moving in direction 120° and is with the vessel.	*Information: tide setting in direction 120 degr. - tide is with you.*
Rate of tidal stream is 1.2 knots and is against the vessel.	*Information: tidal stream one decimal two knots. Tide is against you.*
Rate of the current is 1.4 knots 1 mile N of the breakwater.	*Information: current one decimal four knots in position 1 mile North of breakwater.*
Depth as indicated in the chart must be reduced by 1.2 metre because of the wind.	*Information: charted depth decreased one decimal two metre due to winds.*

(Ref.: annex IMO SMCP p.205)

4.2.2 Vessel transiting a VTS Area

One student will take the role of the Captain replying to Trento Coast Guard.

(❀ 27E Rec 2.6)

MT Delta/ONAZ	Trento Coast Guard
call Trento Coast Guard on VHF Ch 11	
☛ _____ _____ _____	*MT Delta this is Trento Coast Guard.* *Good morning, Captain.* *Advice: Change to VHF Ch 69.* *over*
- call Trento Coast Guard on VHF Ch 69 - inform that you are just passing Trento Light Vessel ☛ _____ _____ _____	*MT Delta this is Trento Coast Guard.* *Question: What is your call sign?* *over*
- answer that your call sign is ONAT - correct your call sign which is ONAZ ☛ _____ _____ _____ _____	*MT Delta/ call sign ONAZ. this is Trento Coast Guard.* *Question 1: What is your position?* *Question 2: What is your course and speed? over*
answer that you are 1 nm S from Trento Light Vessel, you steer 217° at a speed of 12 kn ☛ _____ _____ _____ _____	*MT Delta/ONAZ this is Trento Coast Guard.* *Understood. There is one vessel astern of you, is that correct, Captain?* *over*
confirm that ☛ _____ _____ _____ _____	*MT Delta/ONAZ this is Trento Coast Guard.* *Question 1: What is your port of destination?* *Question 2: What was your last port of call? over*

respond that you come from Antwerp and you are bound for Porto Varnero ☞ _____ _____ _____ _____ _____	MT Delta/ONAZ this is Trento Coast Guard. Last Question: What is your cargo? over
tell the operator that you carry 32,250 metric tons of gas oil ☞ _____ _____ _____ _____	MT Delta/ONAZ this is Trento Coast Guard. I read back cargo : Gas oil 32,250 metric tons. Advice: Call again on VHF Ch 67 when passing Reporting Point 4, Captain. over and out
- inform the operator that this is right - confirm that you will do so - finish the conversation ☞ _____ _____ _____ _____ _____ _____	

4.3 Providing Navigational Assistance Service (NAS)

4.3.1 SMCP Phrases for Providing NAS

(Ref.: annex IMO SMCP pp. 206~208)

Maas Approach (VTS) : information about **Position** of vessel.	SMCP in VHF-communication between VTS- Maas Approach and MV Seaborne - DKEL;
Is land radar service available?	Q : Is shore based Radar assistance available?
Vessel must to report at next waypoint.	Report at next waypoint.
Vessel is closing up to vessel North of her.	Information: you are getting closer to vessel the North of you.
There is a vessel on opposite course that will pass to the Northwest of you.	Information: vessel on opposite course passing to the Northwest of you.
Vessel behind you is going to overtake to the West of you.	Information: vessel following you will overtake to the West of you.
There is crossing traffic in the approach to harbour.	Information: you will meet crossing traffic in the approach to the harbor.
Vessel Southeast of you is at anchor	Information: vessel to the Southeast of you is at anchor.
No 1 Eurobuoy is 2 cables West of you.	Information: No 1 Eurobuoy distance 2 cables to the West of you.
Vessel South of you is going to increase her speed.	Information: vessel to the South of you is increasing speed.
Vessel is proceeding towards fairway limit.	Information: you are approaching limit of fairway.
VTS asks how they get the position	How was your position obtained?
Vessel indicates to VTS that her position was obtained by radar.	Information: my position was obtained by Radar.

VTS asks to repeat her position for identification.	*Repeat your position for identification.*
VTS wants to know what radar-range is used.	*Question: what range scale are you using?.*
Your position was confirmed	*I have located you on my radar screen.*
VTS informs vessel that she is leaving the radar screen.	*Information: you are leaving my screen.*

Maas Approach (VTS) : information about **Course (Track)** of Vessel.	*SMCP in VHF–communication between VTS– Maas Approach and MV Seaborne - DKEL;*
Seaborne's Track is: ● parallel with the reference line. ● moving away from reference line. ● towards the reference line.	*Your track is :* • *parallel with reference line.* • *diverging from reference line.* • *converging to reference line.*
The course that the vessel is steering now is dangerous.	*Warning: you are steering dangerous course.*
Vessel is advised to maintain her present course.	*Advice you keep your present course.*
Vessel is advised to change course to port side.	*Advice you alter course to port.*
Danger!: ● waters North of Seaborne's position are shallow. ● there is an underwater-wreck Northeast of Seaborne's position. ● Seaborne is going to collide with vessel West of her. ● Seaborne is sailing into a fog bank North of her. She must go to emergency anchorage.	*Warning!:* • *You are running into danger! Shallow waters to the North of you.* • *You are running into danger! Submerged wreck to the Northeast of you.* • *You are running into danger! Risk of collision with vessel to the West of you.* • *You are running into danger! Fog bank to the North of you. Instruction: proceed to emergency anchorage".*

| Navy practising in the area Southwest of Baylerock. | *Warning! You are running into danger! Gunnery in progress in area South West of Baylerock.* |
| Vessel is approaching an area that is hidden to view. Other vessels that are approaching must report. | *Information: you are approaching obscured area. Approaching vessels must acknowledge.* |

4.3.2 MT Prima/PQYH calls Simland Traffic

Listen to Simland Traffic(Sweden) from the loudspeaker. Respond to Simland Traffic within the time gaps provided for your responses in the table below. (❀ 10 Rec 3.3)

Simland Traffic	MT Prima/PQYH
MT call sign PQYH this is Simland Traffic. ...	- say the name of your vessel - spell your vessel's name - ask for assistance by RADAR
☞ _____	☞ _____
MT Prima/PQYH this is Simland Traffic. ...	- say that you need to be guided to Simland Port - inform that you are bound for Simland Oil Terminal
☞ _____	☞ _____

MT Prima/PQYH this is Simland Traffic. ...	- answer that you are now at 101° from buoy A3, distance 0.9 nm
☛ _____ _____ _____	☛ _____ _____ _____
MT Prima/PQYH this is Simland Traffic. ...	- respond that you have given a wrong position - correct your position to 101° from buoy A5, distance 0.9 nm
☛ _____ _____ _____ _____	☛ _____ _____ _____ _____
MT Prima/PQYH this is Simland Traffic. ...	- confirm advice given - close the conversation.
☛ _____ _____ _____ _____	☛ _____ _____ _____ _____

4.4 Providing Traffic Organization Service (TOS)

4.4.1 SMCP Phrases for Providing TOS *(Ref.: annex IMO SMCP pp.209-213)*

Maas Approach (VTS) : Information and Instruction about **Arrival, Anchoring, Berthing** of MV Seaborne.	*SMCP in VHF−communication with MV Seaborne − DKEL;*
Vessel is allowed to enter traffic lane at 12:45 UTC and proceed to berth No. 6A.	*Information: You have permission to enter traffic lane at 12:45 hours UTC - traffic clearance granted; proceed to berth number six-alfa.*
Vessel's berth is not ready yet.	*Information: your berth is not clear.*
She is instructed to set course to waiting area. Waiting time is 6 hrs.	*Instruction: you must proceed to waiting berth.* *Information: berthing delayed for 6 hours.*
Anchoring is forbidden outside roadstead.	*Information: anchoring prohibited outside roadstead.*
Vessel must anchor in her present position.	*You must anchor in present position.*
Vessel is not permitted to anchor in present position.	*Do not anchor in present position.*
Vessel must drop her anchors in another position.	*You must anchor in different position.(must anchor clear of fairway)*
Vessel is impeding (hindering) other traffic.	*Information: you are obstructing other traffic.*
Vessel is forbidden to dredge her anchor.	*Do not dredge* anchor.* *(*dredge anchor=인도)*
Vessel in posn 0.5 cable S of roadstead is dragging anchor.	*Information: vessel in position 0.5 cable S of roadstead dragging anchor.*
Vessel must to heave up her anchor.	*You must heave up anchor.*
Vessel is given permission to anchor in her present position and wait for higher tide.	*Information: you have permission to anchor in present position until sufficient water.*
Vessel must go to the anchorage.	*Your orders are to anchor at E-3 anchorage.*

Vessel should move forward / aft 50m.	*Move ahead / astern 50 meters.*
Vessel is in right position- fasten them.	*Your vessel is in position - make fast./*
Vessel is violating traffic rules.	*You are not complying with traffic regulations.*

4.4.2 Cruise Liner Anina/TQ4R arranges Berthing　(❋ 13D Rec 4.2)

Cruise Liner Anina/TQ4R	Gordana Pilot
Establish contact with Gordana Pilot	Advise to go up to VHF Ch 71
☞ _____	☞ _____
Call again on VHF Ch 71 and asks for berthing instructions	Give the following answer : - she will be berthed at Terminal Adria, berth No. C3 - she will be fastened with port side - fenders should be prepared fore and aft - rat guards shall be fixed at all lines Wants to know the ETA at Gordana Pilot Station
☞ _____	☞ _____
Repeat all advice Inform that she will be at Gordana Pilot Station at 12:40 local time, corrects ETA to 11:40 hours local time	Repeat ETA Advise to pick up the pilot in position Gordana Pilot Station at 12:00 hours local time
☞ _____	☞ _____

Confirm advice and say that she has no more questions. Finish the conversation	
☞ _____ _____ _____ _____ _____	

4.4.3 MV Rostock calls Simland Traffic after pilot transfer

(❀ 21E Rec1.5)

MV Rostock/DROS	Simland Traffic
Call Simland Traffic on VHF Ch 22	Ask why she is calling
☞ _____ _____ _____	☞ _____ _____ _____
- Say that the pilot is on board now - Inform that you are about to enter Simland Port - Ask for orders for mooring the ship	- Inform that her berth is Oil Jetty - Tell her that the berth is ready for her at 13:00 hours UTC - Advise that she will be fastened STB'D side
☞ _____ _____ _____ _____ _____ _____	☞ _____ _____ _____ _____ _____ _____
- Confirm the information - Finish the conversation	
☞ _____ _____ _____ _____ _____ _____	

- Call Simland Traffic again - Inform that you are passing by Buoy no. 5 now	Confirm that message
☞ _____ _____ _____ _____ _____	☞ _____ _____ _____ _____ _____
- Call Simland Traffic - Inform that your are now in the Turning Basin North - Inform that you will now turn the ship in order to make fast with STB'D-side	- Confirm this message - Inform that there are no other ships - Permit the ship to turn - Advise to call back when the ship is fast
☞ _____ _____ _____ _____ _____ _____	☞ _____ _____ _____ _____ _____ _____
- Respond that you will call Simland Traffic when the lines are fast	
☞ _____ _____ _____ _____ _____	☞ _____ _____ _____ _____ _____
- Call Simland Traffic again - inform that you are berthed now - Appreciate the help of Simland Traffic - finish the communication	confirm this message
☞ _____ _____ _____ _____ _____	☞ _____ _____ _____ _____ _____

4.5 Handing over to another VTS

(Ref.: annex IMO SMCP p.213)

VTS- handing over of MV Seaborne: Dover Coast Guard to Maas Approach.	SMCP in VHF-communication by VTS- Dover Coastguard and VTS-Maas Approach:
MV Seaborne - DKEL, in position 180 degrees from buoy NH, distance 6.5 miles, working frequency VHF channel 13 is transferred from Dover Coast Guard to Maas Approach.	*MV Seaborne - DKEL, in position bearing 180 degrees from buoy November Hotel, distance 6.5 miles, working frequency VHF channel 13; your target. Please confirm.*
Maas Approach confirms.	*MV Seaborne - DKEL, in position bearing 180 degrees from buoy November Hotel, distance 6.5 miles, working frequency VHF channel 13; my target. I confirm.*

4.6 Communication with Allied Services (Pilot & Tugs)

4.6.1 SMCP Phrases for Pilot request

(Ref.: annex IMO SMCP pp. 214~216)

Pilotage : request by MV Seaborne (call sign DKEL), position: bearing 045 degrees from Alice Buoy, distance 2.5 miles.	SMCP in VHF-communication between MV Seaborne, Pilot Station and pilot boat: VHF-message begins: "ADDRESS & IDENTIFY"
Vessel needs pilot service.	*I require a pilot.* *Information: my posn. bearing 045° from Alice Buoy, distance 2.5 miles.*
Distance between vessel and pilot station is 18.5 miles.	*Information: my distance from pilot station is 18.5 nautical miles.*
Time of arrival at pilot station is 0945 UTC. "	*Information: my ETA at pilot station is 0945 UTC.*
Pilot boat is approaching.	*Information: pilot boat approaching your vessel.*
Vessel does not need pilotage - exemption certificate is on board.	*Information: I do not require a pilot - I am holder of Pilotage Exemption Certificate.*
Pilotage has stopped until further notice.	*Information: pilotage suspended.*
Pilotage will start again at 1400 UTC.	*Information: pilotage is resumed at 1400 UTC.*
Shore based navigational assistance is available.	*Information: shore based navigational assistance available.*
Vessel is given permission to navigate on her own.	*Information: you have permission to proceed by yourself.*
Pilot will come on board at 1350 hrs. UTC.	*Information: pilot will embark at 1350 hrs UTC.*
Vessel must make lee on starboard side.	*You must make lee on your starboard side.*

Vessel must prepare the pilot ladder on starboard side.	*Rig pilot ladder on starboard side.*
Vessel must prepare heaving line and put lights on at pilot ladder.	*Have heaving line ready at pilot ladder; put lights on at pilot ladder.*
Boarding speed is 6 knots.	*Make boarding speed 6 knots.*
It is not possible for the pilot to embark the vessel.	*Information: embarkation not possible.*
Take pilot inside due to high sea.	*Follow the pilot boat inward, where the Pilot will embark.*

4.6.2 Passenger Liner Mandalay/XYZA and Patras Pilot

Listen to the dialogue between a Vessel and a Pilot station, and answer the following questions :   (✿ 2D Rec 1.1)

1	Which station/call sign starts and which station finishes the conversation? ( )
2	Which station is called? ( )
3	What is the working channel of Patras Pilot? ( )
4	Why does the vessel call Patras Pilot? ( )
5	What will be the vessel's berth? ( )
6	Which side will be alongside? ( )

7	What other preparation for berthing is the vessel advised to do? ( )
8	When will the vessel arrive at Patras Pilot Station? ( )
9	At what time will the pilot embark? ( )
10	Which VHF Channel will be used for pilot transfer? ( )

4.6.3 MV Rostock calls the Pilot Boat for pilot transfer

(✿ 20E Rec 1.4)

MV Rostock/DROS	Simland Port Pilot Boat Hermann
Call Simland Port Pilot Boat on VHF Ch 14	Ask MV Rostock/DROS when she will arrive at the Pilot Station
☞ _____ _____ _____ _____	☞ _____ _____ _____ _____
Respond that you will reach the Pilot Station in about 15 minutes.	- Confirm and inform, that you are closing in to MV Rostock/DROS - Order to remain on the current course and to slow down to 6 kn
☞ _____ _____ _____ _____ _____	☞ _____ _____ _____ _____ _____

Repeat the order and say you will do so.	Advise to bring out the pilot ladder on the Stb-side one meter over the water.
☛ _____ _____ _____ _____ _____	☛ _____ _____ _____ _____ _____
Tell the pilot boat that you have brought out the pilot ladder as ordered.	- Warn that the pilot ladder has got damaged steps. - Advise that a new ladder is necessary - repeat this advice.
☛ _____ _____ _____ _____ _____	☛ _____ _____ _____ _____ _____
Inform the pilot boat that you will bring out another pilot ladder on the port side.	- Tell her that this is OK with you - Inform that the pilot will come on board as soon as the other pilot ladder is brought OUT
☛ _____ _____ _____ _____ _____	☛ _____ _____ _____ _____ _____

4.6.4 MT Boris Tolkine/CF9T requires a Pilot

*One cadet acts as the OOW of MT Boris Tolkine responding
to Simland Pilot based on the prompts given, another cadet acts
as Simland Pilot; after that the roles will be swapped.*

(✿ 12D Rec 4.1)

MT Boris Tolkine/CF9T	Simland Pilot
Call Simland Pilot on VHF Ch. 16	Call her via call sign - Advise to change to VHF Ch. 14
☛ _____	☛ _____
Call again on VHF Ch. 14	- Request her to spell her name - Ask what you can do for her
☛ _____	☛ _____
- Spell your vessel's name - Inform that you need a pilot for 15:30 hours local time, Repeat your request	- Ask in what position she is - Ask whether she is underway
☛ _____	☛ _____
- Answer that you are located at Buoy A3 - Confirm that you are underway	You want to know her destination
☛ _____	☛ _____
- Inform that you are bound for the Oil Terminal, berth no.13 - Repeat the information	- You read back the destination - Tell her that the pilot's boarding time will be 1550 hours local - Say that the pilot will embark at Buoy A5
☛ _____	☛ _____

- Request again the time and position the pilot will come on board	- Repeat the boarding time and position of the of the pilot's embarkation - Advise her to change to VHF Ch. 09 for pilot transfer
☞ _____ _____ _____ _____	☞ _____ _____ _____ _____
- Confirm advice - Finish the conversation	
☞ _____ _____ _____ _____	

4.6.5 Create a dialogue between MV Ocean Dance/B4YX and Montego Pilot

The VHF conversation takes place prior to a berthing operation in the port of Montego, first contact has already been established. The shore station Montego Pilot calls MV Ocean Dance/B4YX on the VHF working channel 12.

The shore station tells the vessel that her berth will be Container Terminal 3, berth no. 24.

The vessel asks which side will be alongside.

Montego Pilot responds that the vessel will be expected to make fast port side alongside.

The vessel wants to know the number of tugs required and their arrangements.

Montego Pilot advises that the laws require three tugs and the following arrangements of tugs.

Take:
  - one tug on the port bow
  - one tug on the starboard bow
  - one tug on the starboard quarter

The port radio station advises to use the towing lines of the vessel and to keep the passenger gangway stowed.

Montego Pilot informs the vessel that a gangway will be provided by the port.

The vessel asks what lines are required, and the port radio station responds that the forward lines required are:
  - three head lines
  - two breast lines
  - two forward springs

The aft lines required are:
  - three stern lines
  - two breast lines
  - two aft springs

Montego Pilot also informs the vessel that rat guards to all the lines and springs are prescribed.

The vessel asks where the pilot will come on board.

Montego Pilot advises the vessel to wait for the pilot at Montego Pilot Station and to contact the pilot boat on VHF Channel 09.

Create the dialogue between MV Ocean Dance and Montego Pilot station;

MV Ocean Dance	Montego Pilot
☞	☞
☞	☞
☞	☞
☞	☞
☞	☞
☞	☞
☞	☞
☞	

4.7 VTS Test Demonstration Exercise

This exercise is meant to get you used to one of the possible testing methods. One of you will act as the OOW(Officer Of the Watch) and another one as the VTS Operator.

A vessel (MV Wang Gharay/C9XZ) has reported on to Simland Traffic giving only incomplete data. Create a dialogue with the VTS Centre using the prompts given. Apply the IMO SMCP wherever practicable. Observe the VHF Calling Procedures and Message Markers.

Simland Traffic	MV Wang Gharay/ C9XZ
Call the vessel via her call sign which contacted you on VHF Ch. 16 without giving her name - Ask for her Name and Flag	Call Simland Traffic giving Name/call sign: MV Wang Gharay/C9XZ of New Zealand - Say, that you called on VHF Ch. 16
☛ _____	☛ _____
Advise to go up to VHF Ch. 69	Confirm and do so
☛ _____	☛ _____
Advise to spell the vessel's name	Do as advised
☛ _____	☛ _____
Ask in what position she is	Answer that you are situated 209° from buoy B-1 and 1.7 nm
☛ _____	☛ _____
Ask why she calls	Tell the VTS that you need a pilot
☛ _____	☛ _____
You want to know her destination	Inform that you want to go to Simland Port Container Terminal
☛ _____	☛ _____

You need to know her draft, length o.a. and her gross tonnage	Tell the VTS that your draft is 9.90m, length o.a. 216m, GT 23,400
☞ _____ _____	☞ _____ _____
- Ask what cargo she carries - Ask whether she has dangerous goods on board	Respond that you carry 2,323 20' containers, 4 containers with 240 kg IMO Class 1 on deck included
☞ _____ _____	☞ _____ _____
Request her to repeat the cargo details	Do as requested
☞ _____ _____	☞ _____ _____
- Confirm the cargo details - Ask from what port she comes	Tell the operator that you come from Rotterdam
☞ _____	☞ _____
- Ask when she will reach buoy No. B-3 - Correct your question: You mean buoy No. B-5	- Inform that you will be at buoy No. B-5 at 19:45 local time - Ask where you may pick up the pilot
☞ _____ _____	☞ _____ _____
- Inform that buoy No. B-5 is the position where the pilot will come on board - Tell her that the pilot boat will be there at 19:50 local time	Repeat the information
☞ _____ _____ _____	☞ _____ _____ _____
Advise her to change to VHF Ch. 14 and remain there until the pilot is on board	- Confirm advice - Thank the VTS for its support
☞ _____ _____	☞ _____ _____
Finish the conversation	
☞ _____	

5. CALLING UNKNOWN VESSELS – Identifying positions and vessels

5.1 SMCP Phrases for Inter-Ship Communications

Inter-ship Communication MV Seaborne(DKEL) giving information to Unknown vessel	SMCP in VHF-communication : MV Seaborne to Unknown vessel (=Pearl Head, VRSE):
Address: "All vessels (3X), calling unknown vessel, in position 2 miles South of breakwater" Identity: "This is Seaborne DKEL (3X)"	Address : "Unknown VSL, in position 2 nm South of breakwater Identity : "This is MV Seaborne, DKEL" .....
Seaborne asks unknown vessel about her intentions.	Question: what are your intentions?
Vessel's intention is: • to decrease speed to 4 knots. • to change course to port and steer course 084 degrees.	Intention: I will reduce speed to 4 knots. Intention: I will alter course to port and proceed on course 084 degrees.
• to maintain course and speed.	Intention: I will stand on.
• to continue her voyage and enter Malacca Strait at 13:45 hrs Local time.	Intention: I will proceed and enter Malacca Strait at 13:45 hrs. Local Time.
• to increase speed to 9 knots. • to pass Pulau Karimum-light at 16:50 hrs local time.	Intention: I will increase my speed to 9 knots. Intention: I will pass Pulau Karimum –light at 16:50 hours Local Time.
Seaborne warns unknown vessel that she is steering a dangerous course. • vessel is advised to change course to port side.	Warning!: you are steering dangerous course. Advice: you alter course to port.

Danger!:	Warning! You are running into danger!
• waters ahead of unknown vessel's position are shallow. • there is an underwater-wreck ahead of unknown vessel's position • Unknown vessel is on a collision course with vessel starboard of her.	• Shallow waters ahead of you • Submerged wreck ahead of you. • Risk of collision with vessel on your starboard side.

5.2 Communication between Ship-to-Ship

5.2.1 Identifying positions and vessels

Answer the requests of the calling vessels. In the answer the vessel called will repeat the description given by the calling vessel.   (❀ 22E Rec 2.1)

No.	Calling vessel	Vessel called
1	Unknown ship bearing 198°, distance 4 nm from Cape Sandy, this is MV Dundee/ GB9D on Ch. 16, Come in, please OVER	MV Dundee/GB9D, this is MV Boney King/TY4E. I am the VSL in position bearing 198°, distance 4 nm from Cape Sandy, why do you call OVER
2	Unknown vessel in position 3 nm NE from Flash Point, steering a course of 220°, at a speed of about 8 kn, this is Coast Guard vessel Bell/ P3XX on Ch. 16, Come in, please OVER	MV Seagull Bravo/CFQW ☛ _____ _____ _____ _____ _____ _____ _____

3	Unknown ship, tanker: Hull coloured white with red funnel, steering 066°, speed 11.4 kn, this is MV Clara/D3UT on VHF Ch. 16, Question: How do you read me? Come in, please OVER	MT Cormorant/ZFFQ ☞ _____ _____ _____ _____ _____ _____ _____
4	Unknown vessel, RORO ferry with blue hull and two yellow funnels aft, in position 1.7 nm from Simland Port South entrance, steering NW, this is Indian frigate Bronco/HGGF on Ch. 16, Come in, please OVER	RORO ferry Morrison/K2PP ☞ _____ _____ _____ _____ _____ _____ _____
5	Unknown ship in Brisco Bay, LASH type, steering a course of 008° at a speed of 17kn, this is fishery protection vessel Coddy/LLPO on VHF Ch. 16, Come in, please OVER	LASH vessel Dinghy 2/NCCX ☞ _____ _____ _____ _____ _____ _____ _____
6	Unknown vessel, ocean tug with drilling rig in tow approaching the Traffic Separation Scheme from SE, this is US tall ship Capt. Roy/NV4P on Ch. 16, Come in, please OVER	Ocean tug Mighty/EM7G ☞ _____ _____ _____ _____ _____ _____

5.2.2 Vessels passing one another

The two motor vessels agree on passing one another.

(�֍ 23E Rec 2.2)

MV Buda/HGAR	MV Sandro/IAAU
Call MV Sandro/IAAU • inform her that you will remain your course and speed • tell her that she should pay attention	Answer MV Buda/HGAR, that you - will slow down - will also remain your course - tell her that she may pass on your stb'd-side
☞ _____ _____ _____ _____ _____ _____ _____	☞ _____ _____ _____ _____ _____ _____ _____
• confirm that you will do so, thank her • inform that you remain on VHF Ch. 16 • close the conversation	
☞ _____ _____ _____ _____ _____ _____	

5.2.3 Ship-to-ship general conversation

A motor vessel asks a favour as her radio equipment broke down.

(❀ 26E Rec 2.5)

MV Chantal/CFBZ	MV San Pedro/HQAN
Request the vessel to go to VHF Ch. 10	Call the vessel on VHF Ch. 10 again • ask what the readability is like
☞ _____ _____ _____ _____ _____	☞ _____ _____ _____ _____ _____
• tell her that the signal is very poor • ask what you can do for her	• inform the vessel that your transmitter does not work properly • inform her that you have to transfer a message to Djibouti Radio • ask whether MV Chantal can help
☞ _____ _____ _____ _____ _____	☞ _____ _____ _____ _____ _____
• regret that you cannot help • inform that you are entering the Port of Aden • inform her that you have to handle your own service communications	Tell the officer that you understand this
☞ _____ _____ _____ _____	☞ _____ _____ _____ _____

Wish the officer a good watch and finish conversation	Inform that you will go back to VHF Ch. 16
☛ _____ _____ _____	☛ _____ _____ _____

5.2.4 Identifying ship-to-ship

As the passenger liner is NUC(Not Under Command), she warns the tanker to navigate with caution.　　　(✵ 24E Rec 2.3)

Passenger Liner Tarry Lee/3AAB	Tanker Politayev/UIAG
Call the vessel on your stbd-side, distance 2.3 nm, course 245 °	Answer with name and call sign, • confirm the position • asl why she is calling
☛ _____ _____ _____ _____	☛ _____ _____ _____ _____
• advise her to go up to VHF Ch. 10 • repeat that advice	• call the passenger liner on VHF Ch. 10 • inform her that you are the ship on her stb.-side, distance 2.3 nm
☛ _____ _____ _____	☛ _____ _____ _____
Request the tanker to give her course once again	• confirm your course of 245°
☛ _____ _____ _____ _____	☛ _____ _____ _____ _____

Request her to repeat the course	Repeat your course
☞ _____ _____ _____ _____	☞ _____ _____ _____ _____
• confirm her course • warn the tanker that you are not under command (NUC) • request her to keep a clear distance	• confirm the warning • confirm the request • inform her that you will do as requested
☞ _____ _____ _____ _____ _____ _____	☞ _____ _____ _____ _____ _____ _____
Close the conversation	
☞ _____ _____ _____ _____	

5.3 Identifying vessels and/or their positions in a TSS

This Chart is a schematic arrangement made up for training purposes and does not reflect any real traffic image.

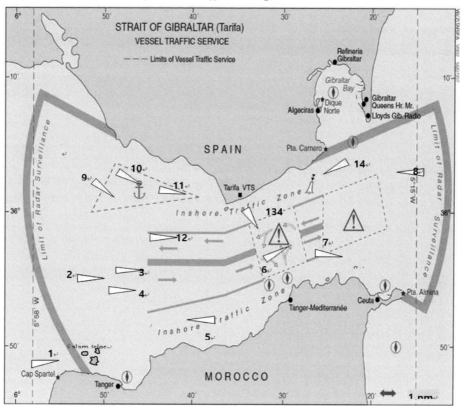

Note: *Eastbound vessels have to communicate with TANGIER TRAFFIC, westbound vessels with TARIFA TRAFFIC*

❋ List of Charted vessels:

1	Seismic Vessel Echo / 5CAG (Mor)	8	Feeder Alison / 9HBB (Mal)
2	PCC Kim Lee Wan / DSAR (Kor)	9	LASH Ramazan / 9YZZ (Tr)
3	Frigate Alain / THAA (F)	10	MV Tanas Palikris / 4JBC (Gr)
4	MV Carmen / YRRD (Rom)	11	CC Takeshi Maru / JAST (J)
5	Fishing Vessel Rybak / RASL(Ru)	12	MT Kazawa / S6AV (Sing)
6	VLCC Merve Karkan / C4AY (Cyp)	13	Passenger Liner Verdi / DWST (G)
7	Tender Malibu / VDNG (Aus)	14	Tall Ship Baltica / SNBF (Pl)

5.3.1 Tangier Traffic calls vessels

One student will read out the part of Tangier Traffic, your partner will act as the OOW of the vessel called responding to the calls of the VTS Centre according to the example given.   (❀ 29E Rec 3.1)

No	Tangier Traffic	Vessel called
1	Vessel in position bearing 260° distance 2 nm from Salam Isles this is Tangier Traffic. Question: What is the name of your vessel and call sign? OVER	*Tangier Traffic this is the vessel in position bearing 260°, distance 2 nm from Salam Isles.* *Answer: The name of my vessel is Echo, call sign 5CAG.* *OVER*
2	Westernmost of the three vessels approaching the S-Lane of the TSS E-bound this is Tangier Traffic. • Question 1: What is the name of your vessel and call sign? • Question 2: What is your flag state? OVER	*Tangier Traffic this is the westernmost vessel of the three vessels approaching the S-Lane of the TSS E-bound.* • *Answer 1: The name of my vessel is PCC Kim Lee Wan, call sign DSAR.* • *Answer 2: My flag state is Korea.* *OVER*
3	Vessel entering the S-Lane of the TSS E-bound close to the Traffic Separation Zone this is Tangier Traffic. • Question 1: What is the name of your vessel and call sign? • Question 2: What type of vessel are you? OVER	☛ _____ _____ _____ _____ _____ _____
4	Vessel southernmost of the three approaching the S-Lane of the TSS E-bound this is Tangier Traffic. • Question: What is the name of your vessel and call sign? OVER	☛ _____ _____ _____ _____ _____ _____ _____

5	Vessel W-bound in the Southern Inshore Traffic Zone this is Tangier Traffic. • Question 1: What is the name of your vessel and call sign? • Question 2: What type of vessel are you? OVER	☞ _____ _____ _____ _____ _____ _____ _____ _____
6	Vessel passing the Round-about E-bound this is Tangier Traffic. Question: What is the name of your vessel and call sign? OVER	☞ _____ _____ _____ _____ _____ _____ _____ _____
7	Vessel leaving the E-bound lane of the TSS passing the SW corner of the Precautionary Area, course 092°, this is Tangier Traffic . • Warning: You are running into danger, shallow water to the SE of you. OVER • Advise her to alter co. to 065 deg.	☞ _____ _____ _____ _____ _____ _____ _____ _____ _____ _____

5.3.2 Vessels are calling Tarifa Traffic

One student will take the part of the OOW of the vessel calling; another student will act as the VTS Operator of Tarifa Traffic according to the example given.

❀ example

No	Vessel calling	Tarifa Traffic
8	*Tarifa Traffic this is Feeder Alison/3HBB Come in, please.* *OVER*	*Feeder call sign 3HBB this is Tarifa Traffic.* *Request: Spell the name of your vessel.* *OVER*
	Tarifa Traffic this is Alison/ 3HBB. *I spell the name of my vessel: Alfa-Lima-India-Sierra-Oscar-November. Alison.* *OVER*	*Alison/3HBB this is Tarifa Traffic.* *Question: What is your position?* *OVER*
	Tarifa Traffic this is Alison/ 3HBB. *Answer: My position is - I am entering the VTS-Area W-bound in position 36°02' N crossing 005°15 W.* *OVER*	*Alison/3HBB this is Tarifa Traffic.* *Information: You have permission to enter the Traffic Lane – traffic clearance granted.* *OVER*

9	(❀ 30E 1 Ramazan)	
Call Tarifa Traffic	**Call her via her call sign and ask what her position is.**	
☛ _____ _____ _____ _____ _____	☛ _____ _____ _____ _____ _____	
Describe your position	**You want to have the ship's name spelt**	
☛ _____ _____ _____ _____ _____	☛ _____ _____ _____ _____ _____	
Spell your ship's name	**Ask her for the reason for calling**	
☛ _____ _____ _____ _____ _____	☛ _____ _____ _____ _____ _____	
Inform the operator that you want to anchor at 10:45 hours UTC	**Respond that she is allowed to do so**	
☛ _____ _____ _____ _____ _____	☛ _____ _____ _____ _____ _____	

10	(✵ 30E 2 Palkins)	
	Call Tarifa Traffic	Address her by her call sign and ask her to advise her position
	☞ _____ _____ _____ _____ _____	☞ _____ _____ _____ _____ _____
	Give the answer required	Request her to spell her ship's name
	☞ _____ _____ _____ _____ _____	☞ _____ _____ _____ _____ _____
	Do as requested	Ask her what she wants you to do
	☞ _____ _____ _____ _____ _____	☞ _____ _____ _____ _____ _____
	Ask when the pilot will come on board	Inform that the pilot will board the ship at13:45 hours local time
	☞ _____ _____ _____ _____	☞ _____ _____ _____ _____

11	(❀ 30E 3 Takeshi)	
	Call Tarifa Traffic	Ask where she presently is
	☞ _____ _____ _____ _____ _____	☞ _____ _____ _____ _____ _____
	• describe your position • inform that you just arrived there • tell her that you wait for a pilot for Tarifa Port	• inform that there will be no pilots at Tarifa Pilot Station until June 06, 14:00 hours LT • advise to keep listening on VHF Ch. 10 and 16
	☞ _____ _____ _____ _____ _____ _____ _____	☞ _____ _____ _____ _____ _____ _____ _____
	Confirm information and advice given	
	☞ _____ _____ _____ _____ _____ _____	

12	(✱ 30E 4 Kazawa)	
	Call Tarifa Traffic	**You want to know her position**
	☞ _____ _____ _____ _____ _____	☞ _____ _____ _____ _____ _____
	Explain what your position is	**You want to have her position once again**
	☞ _____ _____ _____ _____ _____	☞ _____ _____ _____ _____ _____
	Do as requested	• warn that she is using in the wrong traffic lane • tell her that she must sail the Southern Traffic Lane of the TSS • advise her to report to Tangier Traffic on VHF Ch. 69 when in the Southern Traffic Lane
	☞ _____ _____ _____ _____ _____ _____	☞ _____ _____ _____ _____ _____ _____
	Read back the orders given	
	☞ _____ _____ _____ _____ _____ _____	

| 13 | (✿ 30E 5 Verdi)
Make up a dialogue with vessel No.13 together with a partner.
The dialogue should at least comprise three turns.
Vessel No. 13 is making for La Spezia, Italy. |

| 14 | (✵ 30E 6 Baltica)
Make up a dialogue with vessel No. 14 together with a partner.
The dialogue should at least comprise four turns.
Some details of No. 14: course 235°, speed 9.5 kn, power-driven, has to
alter course, VHF Channels to be guarded: 10 and 16. |

6. SHIP REPORTING SYSTEM

There are at least two methods of how to report from ship to shore, that means VTS Stations: Unformatted "free" communication/dialogues or using Ship Reporting Formats which is highly recommended by the IMO. The students have to master both methods, but will realize the advantage of the latter. In all cases, however, the VHF Radio Regulations have to be complied with and the SMCP (Section A/6) whenever practicable.

6.1 Reporting Method

6.1.1 Comparison of the two Methods of reporting to the VTS

Listen to the two dialogues in paras. 6.1.2 and 6.1.3 and fill the blank in the below table.

Compare dialogue 6.1.2 with dialogue 6.1.3 which are based on the same situation	
	How many minutes does it take to exchange the information required?
6.1.2	
6.1.3	
	How many turns are taken to exchange the information required?
6.1.2	
6.1.3	
6.1.3	What is especially saving airtime in this dialogue?
	Discuss the **advantage/disadvantage** *of both methods:* *There is actually only one principal problem ships officers should be aware of:* *Watch Officers tend to transmit more details in a MAREP than really required by the VTS Operators for handling a specific situation. Therefore Code Letters of the Ship Reporting Format which are not necessary to describe the current situation should be omitted from the report. A disadvantage may appear with VTS Operators who do not know or apply the MAREP format, so it is advisable to ask the corresponding VTS Operator whether s/he is prepared to accept a MAREP.*

6.1.2 Unformatted ("free") reporting on at VTS Simland Traffic

(❀ 3D Rec 1.3)

MV Rostock/DROS	VTS Simland Traffic
Simland Traffic this is MV Rostock MV Rostock / DROS on VHF Ch. 22 OVER	MV Rostock / DROS this is Simland Traffic What can I do for you, Captain? OVER
Simland Traffic this is MV Rostock / DROS. *I want to report on, Sir.* *Information: I will enter VTS area Simland Traffic at 241330 hours UTC in position Key South. OVER*	MV Rostock/DROS this is Simland Traffic Question: What is your present position? OVER
Simland Traffic this is MV Rostock / DROS *Answer: My present position is bearing* *122 degrees and 18 nm off Key South. OVER*	MV Rostock/DROS this is Simland Traffic Understood. I have located you on my radar screen. Question: What is your course and speed? OVER
Simland Traffic this is MV Rostock / DROS *Answer: My course is 002 degrees, my speed is 18 knots. OVER*	MV Rostock / DROS this is Simland Traffic Question: What is your port of destination? OVER
Simland Traffic this is MV Rostock / DROS. *Answer: My port of destination is Simland port. OVER*	MV Rostock / DROS this is Simland Traffic Question: What was your last port of call? OVER
Simland Traffic this is MV Rostock / DROS *Answer: My last port of call was Brest, France. OVER*	MV Rostock / DROS this is Simland Traffic Question: What is your gross tonnage? OVER
Simland Traffic this is MV Rostock / DROS *Answer: My gross tonnage is 49,774. OVER*	MV Rostock / DROS this is Simland Traffic Question: What is your present maximum draft, Sir? OVER
Simland Traffic this is MV Rostock / DROS *Answer: My present maximum draft is 11.0 meters. OVER*	MV Rostock / DROS this is Simland Traffic Question: What is your cargo? OVER

Simland Traffic this is MV Rostock / DROS. *Answer: My cargo is 3,473 20' containers, no dangerous goods. OVER*	*MV Rostock / DROS this is Simland Traffic.* *Question: Do you have any restrictions? OVER*
Simland Traffic this is MV Rostock / DROS *Answer: No, I have no restrictions. OVER*	*MV Rostock / DROS this is Simland Traffic* *Question: Who is your agent in Simland Port? OVER*
Simland Traffic this is MV Rostock / DROS *Answer: My agent in Simland Port is SimTrans Ltd. OVER*	*MV Rostock / DROS this is Simland Traffic* *Information: Pilotage is compulsory.* *Advice: Contact Simland Pilot on VHF Channel 14. OVER*
Simland Traffic this is MV Rostock / DROS *Understood. I will contact Simland Pilot on VHF Ch. 14.* *Thank you for your assistance and good watch. OUT.*	

6.1.3 Formatted reporting on at VTS Simland Traffic

(�֍ 4D Rec 1.4)

MV Rostock/DROS	VTS Simland Traffic
Simland Traffic this is MV Rostock MV Rostock / DROS on VHF Ch. 22 over	MV Rostock / DROS this is Simland Traffic. - What can I do for you, Captain? over
Simland Traffic this is MV Rostock / DROS I want to give my MAREP Position Report. OVER	MV Rostock / DROS this is Simland Traffic. Understood. Go ahead with your MAREP POSREP. OVER
Simland Traffic this is MV Rostock / DROS Listen to my MAREP POSREP. - Alfa: MV Rostock, call sign DROS, flag state Germany - Bravo: 241200 hours UTC - Delta: bearing 122 degrees, distance 18 nm off Key South - Echo: 002 - Foxtrot: 180 - Golf: Brest, France - Hotel: 241330 - India: Simland Port, ETA 250715 local time - Mike: VHF Ch. 16 and 11 guarded, 2182 kHz guarded, Inmarsat B and C operational - Oscar: 1100 - Papa: 3,473 20' containers, no dangerous goods. - Quebec: No restrictions - Tango: Simtrans Ltd. - Zulu: End of report. over	MV Rostock / DROS this is Simland Traffic. - Received your MAREP POSREP. - Information: Pilotage is compulsory. - Advice: Change to VHF Ch. 14, Captain. OVER
Simland Traffic this is MV Rostock/DROS - Understood. Changing to Simland Pilot on VHF Ch. 14. - Thank you for your assistance, and good watch. OUT	

6.2 The Standard Reporting Format MAREP

More details of MAREP will be found in IMO Resolution A.851(20).

"Free" dialogues will occasionally be preferred by VTS Operators instead of using MAREP (though the latter is recommended by IMO and IALA).

As OOWs tend to transmit more details in a MAREP than really required by the VTS Operators for a specific situation. Therefore Code Letters of the Ship Reporting Format which are not necessary to describe the current situation should be omitted from the report. Certain VTS Centers require OOWs to apply the MAREP format. The IMO SMCP should be used wherever possible.

6.2.1 Abbreviation used in the MAREP

Sailing Plan (SP)	Before or as near as possible to the time of departure from a port within a system or when entering the area covered by a system.
Position Report (PR)	When necessary to ensure effective operation of the system.
Deviation Report (DR)	When the ship's position varies significantly from the position that would have been predicted from previous reports, when changing the reported route, or as decided by the master.
Final Report (FR)	On arrival at destination and when leaving an area covered by the system.
Dangerous Goods Report (DG)	When an incident takes place involving the loss or likely loss overboard of packaged dangerous goods, including those in freight containers, portable tanks, road and rail vehicles and shipborne barges, into the sea.
Harmful Substances Report (HS)	When an incident takes place involving the discharge or probable discharge of oil (Annex I, MARPOL 73 / 78) or noxious liquid substances in bulk (Annex II, MARPOL 73 / 78).

Marine Pollutants Report (MP)	In the case of loss overboard of harmful substances in packaged form including those in freight containers, portable tanks, road and rail vehicles and shipborne barges, identified in the IMDG Code as marine pollutants (Annex III, MARPOL 73 / 78).
Any other report	Any other report should be made according to the requirements set by the corresponding Government.

6.2.2

6.2.3 MAREP Format

Telegraphy	Telephone (alternative)	Function	Information required
Name of system (e.g.**AMVER**/ MASTREP/ MAREP/ ECAREG/ JASREP)	Name of system (e.g.**AMVER** / MUSTREP / MAREP / ECAREG / JASREP)	System identifier	Ship reporting system or nearest appropriate coast radio station
	State in full	Type of report	Type of report:
SP			Sailing Plan
PR			Position Report
DR			Deviation Report
FR			Final Report
DG			Dangerous Goods Report
HS			Harmful Substances Report
MP			Marine Pollutants Report
Give in full			Any other report

A (Alfa)	Ship	Ship	Name, call sign or ship station identity, and flag
B (Bravo)	Time	Date and time of event	A 6 digit group giving day of month (first two digits), hour and minutes (last four digits).
C (Charlie)	Position	Position	A 4 digit group giving latitude (N or S) and a 5 digit group giving longitude(E-East or W-West)
D (Delta)	Position	Position	True bearing (first 3 digits) and distance (state distance) in nautical miles from a clearly identified landmark (state landmark)
E (Echo)	Course	True Course	A 3 digit group
F (Foxtrot)	Speed	Speed in knots & tenths of knots	A 3 digit group
G (Golf)	Departed	Port of departure	Name of last port of call
H (Hotel)	Entry	Date, time and point of entry into system	Entry time expressed as in (B) and entry position expressed as in (C) or (D)
I (India)	Destination and ETA	Destination and expected time of arrival	Name of port and date and time, expressed as in (B)
J (Juliet)	Pilot	Pilot	State whether a deep sea or a local pilot is on board

K (Kilo)	Exit	Date, time and point of exit from system or arrival at the ship's destination	Exit time expressed as in (B) and exit position expressed as in (C) or (D)
L (Lima)	Route	Route information	Intended track
M (Mike)	Radio-communications	Radiocomm-unications	Sate in full names of stations/ frequencies guarded
N (November)	Next report	Time of next report	Date time group expressed as in (B)
O (Oscar)	Draft	Maximum present static draft in metres	4 digit group giving metres and centimetres
P (Papa)	Cargo	Cargo on board	Cargo and brief details of any dangerous goods
Q (Quebec)	Defect, damage, deficiency, limitations	Defects/ damage/ deficiencies/ other limitations	Brief details of defects, damage, deficiencies or other limitations
R (Romeo)	Pollution / dangerous goods lost overboard	Description of pollution or dangerous goods lost overboard	Brief details of type of pollution (oil, chemicals, etc.), or dangerous goods lost overboard; positions expressed as in (C) or (D)
S (Sierra)	Weather	Weather conditions	Brief details of weather and sea conditions
T (Tango)	Agent	Ship's representa-tive and/or owner	Details of name and particulars of ship's representative or owner

U (Uniform)	Size and type	Ship size and type	Details of length, breadth, tonnage, and type, etc. as required
V (Victor)	Medic	Medical personnel	Doctor, physician's assistant, nurse, personnel with medical training
W (Whisky)	Persons	Total number of persons on board	State number
X (X-ray)	Remarks	Miscellaneous	Any other information
Y (Yankee)	Relay	Request to relay report to another system	Content of report
Z (Zulu)	End of report	End of report	No further information required [12)]

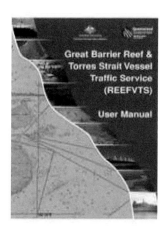

Also, beside radio communication, some Authorities require Ships to report in accordance with specific formats via Ship's e-mail or InMarSat system.

Therefore it is required for Mariners to refer to appropriate Publications & Guidelines (Radio signal, Local publications) as some regulations are very strict about false or missing reports. (e.g. Australia)

---

12) **IMO Resolution A.851(20)**, Adopted on 27 November 1997, "General Principles for Ship Reporting Systems and Ship Reporting Requirements, including Guidelines for reporting Incidents involving Dangerous Goods, Harmful Substances and/or Marine Pollutants.

6.2.4 AMVER

Automated
Mutual-assistance
VEssel-Rescue (system)

AMVER, sponsored by the US Coast Guard, is a free, computer-based and voluntary ship reporting system used worldwide by SAR authorities to arrange for assistance in distress at sea. (www.amver.com)

With AMVER, rescue coordinators can identify participating vessels in the area of distress and divert the best‒positioned ship or ships to respond.

Participating in AMVER does not put ships under any additional obligation to assist in SAR operations beyond that which is required under international law.

Saving Lives At Sea since 1966

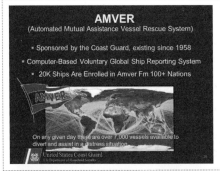

6.2.5 Reporting Practice

The tasks should be done as role plays: one student will act as the OOW, the other as the Operator in the VTS Station asking corresponding questions or giving advice. Send the following messages to VTS Stations with MAREP Format.

(✸ 5D Rec 3.1)

No.	Information
	First contacts to the VTS Stations have already been established
1	Calling station: German LG Tanker Thor/DLKF Station called: Pauline Traffic Gross tonnage: 3,205 Date and time: 261230 hrs local time without a pilot Position at 261230 hrs LT 51-22 N, 002-01 E Entering the area: 261400 hours local time at Reporting Point Bravo 1 Course 074°, speed 14 kn Destination: Trieste, Italy Cargo: liquefied Ammoniac, 2,430 t Draft: 3.5 m VHF Ch. guarded: 69, 16 Leaving the area: 270014 hours local time in position Reporting Point Golf 3 Agent in Trieste : Trans Gas Co.
Alfa Bravo Charlie Echo Foxtrot	

Hotel India Juliet Kilo Mike Oscar Papa Quebec Tango Uniform Zulu	
3	Calling station: VLCC Ylva/S4DS Station called: Vonda Traffic Flag: Sweden Date and time: 280400 hours UTC Position: 4.8 nm NNW of Terra Rossa Speed: 18 kn, course 122° true Destination: Rijeka, Croatia, Outer Roads, ETA 301030 hours UTC Cargo: 282,000 mt of crude oil Type of ship: Very Large Crude Carrier Draft: 19.33 m Exit from VTS area: 281130 hours UTC in position Reporting Point Alfa 2

Alfa	
Bravo	
Delta	
Echo	
Foxtrot	
India	
Kilo	
Oscar	
Papa	
Quebec	
Uniform	
Zulu	

7. DISTRESS, URGENCY AND SAFETY COMMUNICATIONS

It is of utmost importance to comply with the Radio Regulations regarding Distress, Urgency and Safety Communications. Violating the Regulations may lead to wasting valuable time, loss of property, environmental pollution and even to loss of lives. The type of vessel, e.g. Motor Vessel (MV), Ferry or Motor Tanker etc. has not necessarily to be mentioned in these communications in order to keep messages as short as possible.

7.1 Scheme for a Distress Call/Message

Transmission of a Distress Call and a Distress Message International Distress and Calling Frequencies: VHF Channel 16 = 156.8 MHz and 2182 kHz
MAYDAY indicates that a ship, an aircraft, or other vehicle or a person is threatened by grave and imminent danger and requires immediate assistance. **Note:** In the DSC a Distress Alert made on the appropriate frequency/VHF Ch. 70 is automatically sent.
Distress Call
MAYDAY   (3x) **this is** **name of the vessel in distress**   (3x) **call sign** (MMSI* if the alert was sent by DSC**)
Distress Message

MAYDAY
name of the vessel in distress
call sign (MMSI if the alert was sent by DSC)
+   position
+   nature of distress
+   assistance required
+   any other useful information, such as:
       - Master's intention
       - type of cargo (if dangerous)
       - weather and sea condition
       - time of abandonment
       - number and type of survival craft launched
       - number of persons abandoning/staying on board
over

* MMSI = Maritime Mobile Service   ** DSC = Digital Selective Calling

Acknowledgement of a Distress Message

A vessel, upon receiving a distress call/message from another vessel in vicinity <u>should acknowledge receipt immediately</u> unless in sea areas A1/A2*, time about 5 minutes should be given for a coast station/MRCC to acknowledge. Where the station in distress is a long distance away, then acknowledge or relay to the nearest coast station/MRCC only if no other acknowledgement has been heard.

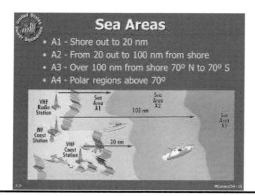

MAYDAY

name/call sign of the vessel in distress

this is

name/call sign of the acknowledging station

received MAYDAY

Having acknowledged the distress call then continue as follows:

MAYDAY

name of the vessel in distress   (3x)

call sign

this is

name of assisting vessel   (3x)

call sign

+ position of assisting vessel

+ speed to distress position

+ ETA at distress position

(if advisable: bearing of the vessel in distress)

OVER

7.2 SMCP Phrases for DISTRESS Communications

(Ref.: IMO SMCP pp. 178~187)

DISTRESS MV Seaborne (DKEL, MMSI 235786000): Position 69-29N / 042-53E. December 14 – 1345hrs UTC	*SMCP in VHF-communication : her DSC-alert has been acknowledged; VHF-message begins: MAYDAY + ID + POS*
The whole ship is on fire. There is danger that the vessel will explode.	*I am on fire in posn.69 degr.29 min. N / 042 degr. 53 min E.; danger of explosion*
Fire has been located in the engine room and in the superstructure.	*Fire is in engine room and in superstructure .*
Fire has been detected in no. 2 hold. The smoke is poisonous.	*Fire is in number-2 hold; smoke toxic.*
Vessel is unmanoeuverable.	*I am not under command (NUC).*
Fire cannot be extinguished by vessel's own equipment.	*Fire not under control; I require fire fighting assistance.*
Six crew members have been injured.	*Number of injured persons: six.*
Two crew members were killed.	*Number of casualties: two.*
Water is entering the ship below the waterline.	*I am flooding below waterline.*
Vessel is heeling over 20 degrees to port side; deck cargo will be put overboard.	*I have a dangerous list to port; I will jettison cargo to stop listing.*
Vessel is unable to continue her voyage. Tug assistance is needed.	*I am not under command; I require tug assistance.*
Vessel has had a collision with an unknown object.	*I have collided with unknown object.*
The crew are leaving the vessel after the vessel has had a collision.	*Crew must abandon vessel after collision".*
Vessel is damaged below waterline, but she is able to continue her voyage without assistance.	*I have damage below waterline; I can proceed without assistance.*
Vessel is sinking after an explosion.	*I am sinking after explosion*

Vessel is adrift.	*I am adrift.*
Vessel is aground and needs tug assistance. Refloating expected when tide gets higher.	*I am aground; I require tug assistance. I expect to refloat when tide rises.*
Vessel is being attacked by pirates. No damage has been caused to the ship. Vessel will continue her voyage.	*I am under attack of pirates. I have no damage; I will proceed.*
Someone has fallen overboard.	*I have lost person overboard in position 69° 29′ N / 042° 53′ E.*

DISTRESS MV Seaborne(DKEL, MMSI 235786000): Position 69-29N / 042-53E. Require **Medical Assistance**	*SMCP in VHF-communication: between MV Seaborne and RCC* Kola Radio;VHF-message begins: MAYDAY + ID + POS* ** Rescue Coordination Center*
Vessel requests for medical assistance.	*I require medical assistance.*
Vessel requests for helicopter with doctor.	*I require helicopter with doctor.*
Message from RCC: helicopter is airborne and on its way.	*Message from RCC: Information: helicopter is on the way.*
Helicopter will arrive in distress position within 1 hour.	*Information: helicopter ETA distress position within one hour.*
Helicopter will use rescue sling.	*Information: I will use rescue sling.*
Relative wind direction is 045 degrees at 26 knots.	*Information: relative wind zero four five degrees, speed is two six knots.*
Vessel indicates that all is clear for landing.	*Information: I am ready to receive you.*
Patient cannot be taken from board.	*Information: transfer of patient not possible.*
<Search & Rescue Unit Vendor is underway to assist MV Seaborne>	*<SRU Communication between SRU, MV Seaborne and Vessels>*

SRU Vendor will be the on-scene-coordinator.	*Information: I will act as on-scene-Coordinator.*
Vendor displays an orange flag and two red vertical lights.	*Information: I will show following signals: orange flag - two red vertical lights.*
SRU is underway to distress position to render assistance. Her position is 69° 29′N / 030° 53′E., her course is 135°; her speed is 12 knots. ETA within 1 hour.	*Information: I am proceeding to your assistance; my position 69° 29′ N / 030° 53′ E., my course is 135°; my speed is one two knots; my ETA distress position within one hour.*
Request to all ships to assist with search for missing person and report any result to On-Scene Co-ordinator.	*Request: all vessels in vicinity of position 69° 29′ N / 042° 53′ E: keep sharp lookout and report to On-Scene- Coordinator.*
Weather in distress position: wind SW 3; visibility is moderate; sea is smooth; current 2.5 knots to SW.	*Information: wind SW Beaufort force three; visibility moderate; smooth; current two decimal five knots to SW.*
End of SAR operations. The search for missing person is stopped; no one was found.	*We finish with SAR-operations. Vessels have permission to stop search and proceed with voyage; result of search negative.*

7.2.1 Example of a Distress Call/Message (MAYDAY Message and Acknowledgement)

(✼ 31F Rec 1.2)

MAYDAY   MAYDAY   MAYDAY *this is Ringo   Ringo   Ringo   call sign PPAY*
MAYDAY Ringo / PPAY ***Position** 62° 11.8' North, 007° 44' East.* ***I am on fire** after explosion in engine room.* *I am not under command.* *Fire is not under control.* ***I require fire fighting assistance.*** ***My cargo is wood pulp.*** *I have launched one lifeboat with 8 persons.* *3 officers and master staying on board.* *Warning: Many sailing yachts near distress position.   over*

Acknowledgement:

More than 5 minutes elapsed and no acknowledgement from a coastal station or MRCC* was heard.
MAYDAY Ringo / PPAY this is Cindy / V3AF ***received MAYDAY***
MAYDAY *Ringo   Ringo   Ringo / PPAY* *this is Cindy   Cindy   Cindy / V3AF* ***Position** 8.5 nm SW of distress position.* ***Speed** 18 kn.* ***ETA** at distress position within 50 minutes.   OVER*

* MRCC = Maritime Rescue Coordination Center.

Cases of Distress as given in the GMDSS (via DSC Alert)	
1　Fire/explosion	7　Disabled and adrift
2　Flooding	8　Undesignated distress
3　Collision	9　Abandoning vessel
4　Grounding	10　Piracy/Armed attack
5　Listing/Danger of capsizing	11　Person over board
6　Sinking	12　EPIRB emission

<Example of Medical Assistance>　(※ 77 F Rec 4.2)

MV Bruni/IAGV	Medico Fortas
PAN-PAN (3x) Medico Fortas (3x) this is MV Bruni (3x) call sign IAGV. I require medical assistance. OVER	MV Bruni/IAGV this is Medico Fortas. Advice: Change to VHF Ch. 28. OVER
Medico Fortas this is MV Bruni/IAGV. Understood. Changing to VHF Ch. 28. OVER	No reply
Medico Fortas this is MV Bruni/IAGV on VHF Ch. 28. OVER	MV Bruni/IAGV this is Medico Fortas. Question: What kind of assistance is required? OVER
Medico Fortas this is MV Bruni/IAGV. Answer: I require helicopter with doctor for a female with suspected appendicitis. OVER	MV Bruni/IAGV this is Medico Fortas. Question: What is your position? OVER
Medico Fortas this is MV Bruni/IAGV. Answer: My position is bearing 034°, distance 9.2 nm from Fagasta Banks. OVER	MV Bruni/IAGV this is Medico Fortas. Information: I will send a helicopter with doctor - ETA within 35 minutes. Advice: Change to VHF Ch. 26 for communication with helicopter. OVER
Medico Fortas, this is MV Bruni/IAGV. Understood: I will Change to VHF Ch. 26 for communication with helicopter. OUT	

7.2.2 Relaying scheme of a Distress Message

Distress Message by a Station NOT itself in Distress
This message will be sent • *when a distress alert/call is not acknowledged by a coast station or another vessel within 5 minutes* • *when the station in distress is unable of participating in distress communications* • *if the person responsible for the vessel not in distress considers that further help is necessary.*
Distress call
MAYDAY RELAY   (3x) **all stations (or a specific coast station)**   (3x) **this is** **name of relaying station**   (3x) **call sign** (or MMSI if the alert was sent by DSC)
Relayed message

At … hours UTC on VHF Ch. 16 or frequency …
following received:
<u>begins</u>
MAYDAY name/call sign of the vessel in distress
          + unchanged text of the distress message received
<u>ends</u>
 	
or:
MAYDAY my position: ....
following observed: ....
this is name/call sign of relaying station*
                              over
 	
  * *This sentence is not covered by Regulations, but it proved to be useful in the practice of radio communication*

7.2.3 Examples of relayed Distress Messages

(✽ 32F Rec 1.7)

MAYDAY RELAY   MAYDAY RELAY   MAYDAY RELAY

ALL STATIONS   ALL STATIONS   ALL STATIONS

this is Cindy Cindy Cindy / V3AF

At 13:45 hours UTC on VHF Channel 16 following received
– begins:
MAYDAY
Ringo / PPAY
Position 62° 11.8' North, 007° 44' East.
I am on fire after explosion in engine room.
I am not under command.
Fire is not under control.
I require fire fighting assistance.
My cargo is wood pulp.
I have launched one lifeboat with 8 persons.
3 officers and master staying on board.
Warning: Many sailing yachts near distress position
– ends.
This is Cindy/V3AF.   over

Or:

MAYDAY RELAY   MAYDAY RELAY   MAYDAY RELAY

MRCC Adriata   MRCC Adriata   MRCC Adriata

this is Tasco Tasco Tasco / P3AS

MAYDAY
My position 45° 12.55' North, 014° 33.24' East
At 09:23 hours UTC following observed:
Single-engined airplane type Cessna on fire crashed into the sea
– no mayday heard.
This is Tasco / P3AS.   over

7.3 Urgency and Safety Communication schemes

Urgency / Safety Communication

The message is announced on VHF Ch. 16 and then transmitted on a ship-to-ship channel. Short messages may be transmitted on VHF Ch. 16, this channel may also be used when the transmission on a ship-to-ship Channel is not practicable. Messages to Coastal Radio Stations are transmitted on VHF Channel 16, which then – if necessary -will announce a working Channel for further Urgency/Safety communication.

PAN-PAN   means that the calling station has an **urgent message** concerning the **safety of a ship, an aircraft or other vehicle or a person.**

SECURITE   means that the calling station has a **message** concerning the **safety of navigation** or giving **important meteorological warnings.**

Urgency / Safety Call

PAN - PAN   or   SECURITE   (3x)

all stations or a specific station   (3x)

this is

name of transmitting station   (3x)
call sign (MMSI if the alert was sent by   DSC)

Advice: Listen on VHF Channel ...   OVER

Urgency / Safety Message

PAN - PAN   or   SECURITE   (3x)

all stations or a specific station   (3x)

this is

name of transmitting station   (3x)
call sign (MMSI if the alert was sent by DSC)

text of the Urgency or Safety Message

OVER and OUT

Note: These types of priority calls are similar to Distress Calls. That means, in Urgency/Safety communications, after having established contact to the station called, the Urgency/Safety Signal at the beginning of the Urgency/Safety Call is no longer used. Urgency communications in SAR operations need not necessarily be preceded by the Urgency Signal to facilitate the exchange of information.

7.3.1 SMCP Phrases for URGENCY / SAFETY Communications

(Ref.: annex IMO SMCP pp. 127~133)

URGENCY MV Seaborne(DKEL, MMSI 235786000): Position 69-29N / 042-53E.	*SMCP in VHF-communication : her DSC-alerr has been acknowledged; VHF-message begins: PAN-PAN PAN-PAN PAN-PAN, All stations(3X) +ID+ POS*
Vessel is unmanoeuverable due to problems with main engine.	*I am not under command; I have problems with main engine.*
Other traffic in the vicinity is asked to keep clear.	*Request all vessels keep clear.*
Tug assistance is needed.	*I require tug assistance.*
Vessel has problems with her manoeuverability due to problems with her steering gear.	*I am manoeuvering with difficulty; I have problems with steering gear.*
Vessel is losing dangerous substance (IMO-class 6).	*I am spilling dangerous goods of IMO- class 6, in position 69°29' N/ 042°53' E.*
There is immediate risk of pollution.	*Warning: danger of pollution imminent.*
Request for assistance to clear oil.	*I require oil clearance assistance.*
Vessel has problems with her stability due to heavy icing.	*I have stability problems - heavy icing.*
SAFETY Weather, Hydrography, Ice & etc. Message by VTS station	*SMCP in VHF-communication : VHF-message begins: SECURITE(3X), All stations(3X) + ID + Time*
Winds from SW force 4 are expected to increase to force 7 in White Sea area.	*Warning: wind direction SW force Beaufort four, expected to increase force seven in White Sea area.*
Barometer will fall quickly.	*Warning: barometer dropping rapidly.*
Maximum winds of 50 knots are expected.	*Warning: maximum winds of five zero knots expected.*
Swell of 3 metres from SW is expected in White Sea area within the next hour.	*Warning: swell of 3 metres from SW expected in White Sea area within next hour.*

Freak wave is expected by 23.45 UTC in posn 69 degr. 29 min. N 1042 degr. 53 min E.	*Warning: Tsunami expected by 23.45 UTC in posn. 69 degr.29 min. N / 042 degr. 53 min E.*
The tide is 2 metres higher than expected.	*Warning: tide 2 metres above prediction.*
Abnormally low water is expected within 6 hours.	*Warning: abnormally low water expected within 6 hours. within 6 hrs.*
Water is not deep enough.	*Warning: depth of water not sufficient.*
Depth indicated in the chart must be reduced by 1.5 metre because of the sea state.	*Warning: charted depth of water decreased by one decimal five metre due to sea state.*
Visibility is reduced due to fog.	*Warning: visibility restricted by fog.*
Visibility will be decreased to 50 metres.	*Information: visibility expected to decrease to five zero metres.*
Ice warning: an iceberg has been located in posn 69 degr. 29 min. N I 042 degr. 53 min E.	*Ice warning: iceberg located in posn. 69 degr.29 min. N / 042 degr. 53 min E.*
We expect that the ice situation N of White Sea area will deteriorate.	*Warning: ice situation expected to deteriorate N of White Sea area.*
We expect that the thickness of the ice will increase.	*Information: thickness of ice expected to increase.*
<SAFETY: Buoyage & Obstruction>	*<SAFETY: Same Procedure>*
Buoy KL 2 in vicinity of posn. 69 degr. 29min. N / 042 degr 53 min E. is no longer in its correct position.	*Warning: Buoy Kilo Lima two in posn. 69 degr.29 min. N / 042 degr. 53 min E. off station.*
Buoy KL 2 in vicinity of posn. 69 degr. 29 min. N / 042 degr 53 min E. is missing.	*Warning: Buoy Kilo Lima two in posn. 69 degr. 29 min. N / 042 degr. 53 min E. missing.*
No light on CA4-buoy in posn. 69 degr. 29 min. N / 042 degr. 53 min E	*Warning: buoy Charlie Alfa-four in posn. 69 degr. 29 min. N / 042 degr.53 min E unlit.*

AL2-buoy in posn. 69 degr. 29 min. N / *042* degr. 53 min E deg. 53 min. E. is unreliable.	*Warning: buoy Alfa Lima two, in posn. 69 degr.29 min. N / 042 degr. 53 min E is unreliable".*
We have detected a mine adrift in posn. 69 degr.29 min. N / *042* degr. 53 min E.	*Warning: mine adrift in vicinity of posn. 69 degr. 29 min. N / 042 degr.53 min E.*
We have detected an unlit derelict vessel adrift in posn. 69 degr.29 min. N / *042* degr. 53 min E.	*Warning: unlit derelict vessel adrift in vicinity of posn. 69 degr.29 min. N / 042 degr. 53 min E.*
We have detected a shoal in posn. 69 degr. 29 min. N / 042 degr. 53 min E. that has not been charted yet.	*Warning: uncharted shoal reported in posn. 69 degr. 29 min. N / 042 degr. 53 min E.*
We have detected an obstruction in posn. 69 degr. 29 min. N / *042* degr. 53 min E. (confirmed).	*Warning: obstruction located in posn. 69 degr. 29 min. N / 042 degr. 53 min E".*
We are performing dangerous operation in posn. 69 degr. 29 min. N / 042 degr. 53 min E. Traffic is requested to keep distance from us.	*Warning: hazardous operations in posn. 69 degr. 29 min. N / 042 degr. 53 min E. Wide berth requested.*

7.3.2 Examples of Urgency and Safety Messages

The following messages are regarded as short messages.

(❀ 33F Rec 1.8)

.1 Urgency Message

PAN-PAN   PAN-PAN   PAN-PAN
ALL STATIONS ALL STATIONS ALL STATIONS
this is Passenger Liner Otero Otero Otero / HOAA

Position 19° 55.6' North and 091° 31' West.
I have problems with engines.
I am not under command.
I am drifting SSE.
Persons on board : 824
I require urgently tug assistance.
OVER

.2 Safety Message:

In most cases SAFETY communications are **"one-way" transmissions,** i.e. no verbal response is expected from ships having received a Safety Message. That is why those messages **mostly end with "out".** In quite a few cases the transmitting stations do not introduce a Safety Message with the Safety Signal **SECURITE**, but with the announcement "**Navigational warning** (no. ...)", "Warning to navigation in area ...", "**Meteorological warning** for ..." or the like.

SECURITE   SECURITE   SECURITE
BELO BAY RADIO   BELO BAY RADIO   BELO BAY RADIO
this is Naval Tender   Libertad Libertad Libertad / CPFG

Uncharted dangerous wreck located in position bearing 212°, distance 4.9 nm from Belo Reef.
  OUT

7.4 Priority Communication Practices

7.4.1 Draft a corresponding Priority Message (Distress/ Urgency/ Safety)

1	Calling station: MV Martin / DMAR ✵ 65F Rec 2.3-1 Station called: RCC Sarota Situation: - your propeller is foul due to a twisted fishing net - you have no chance to manoeuver the ship - you are going to drift at 0.8 kn to SSE - you are situated 4.8 nm south of the Isle of Sarota - you need to be helped by tugboats
2	Calling station: MV Bonny / GBON ✵ 66F Rec 2.3-2 Situation: - a child dropped over board with a life jacket on - this happened at 09:35 hours local time - it happened in position 011° and 11.6 nm from Sandy Shallows - vessels should be aware of sand banks which are not marked in the charts
3	Calling station: Trento Traffic ✵ 67F Rec 2.3-3 Situation: - a pipeline got damaged and emits gas in position 3 nm S of Santano Reef - mariners are recommended to pass the position windward and at a safe distance - vessels are warned of danger of explosion Date and time: June 21 16:30 hours UTC

4	Calling station: VLCC Exxon Blue / AEXX ✿ 68F Rec 2.3-4
	Situation:
	- you bumped into an unidentified object in position 53°57.05' N and 125°34.85 E
	- the tanker cannot be manoeuverd
	- your ship is drifting at a speed of 0.75 kn to SSW
	- you carry 122,760 t of crude oil
	- you need the help of tugs
	- attention: There is an oil rig without lights ca 7 nm W from your position
5	Calling station: MV Candy / C6UL ✿ 69F Rec 2.3-5
	- you send a call on VHF Ch. 16
	- then ask vessels to switch to VHF Ch. 13
	- you send the corresponding message
	Situation:
	- 16 containers (20') dropped over board in position 53 22 S 163 18 W
	- time of the incident: March 28, 13:50 hours UTC
	- containers set to NNW
	- warning: 4 containers are full with IMO Class 6.1 – danger to the environment
	- warning: Drifting containers may be danger to shipping
6	Calling station: MV Dora Santos/4DOR ✿ 70F Rec 2.3-6
	Situation:
	- a fire developed in no. 1 hold loaded with cotton
	- fire is gaining headway to aft
	- thick smoke coming out of no. 1 hold – not toxic
	- help to extinguish the fire urgently needed
	- you are in position 005°, 6.45 nm west of Shellfish Banks
	- warning: there are many small fishing boats showing not lights at all

7	Calling station: Marina Delgado ✵ 71F Rec 2.3-7
	Situation:
	- a sailing yacht named Belinda left Flores on the 13th at 09:30 hours UTC
	- she left for the Marina Saluta and was expected to arrive at 16:00 hours UTC
	- she did not show up there until now
	- yacht has a blue hull and two masts with light yellow sails, she is 27 m long
	- there are six persons on board
	- sightings should be reported to MRCC Azores
8	Calling station: MV Hebab / 6GFB ✵ 72F Rec 2.3-8
	Station called: Hitashi Radio
	Situation: The approaching buoy to Hitashi Port, i.e. A7, is not in its charted position

7.5 Hearing Practices for various Accent

The majority of radio messages recorded has on purpose been spoken by non-native English speakers as future navigational officers will mainly be exposed to a communication environment where English is used as a foreign language.

Listen to the following messages and write down if you find messages not complying with the VHF Regulations.

Reception of Distress, Urgency, Safety Messages and Navigational Warnings
MAYDAY (3x) this is passenger vessel Morsh (3x) R7OX Mayday passenger vessel Morsh / R7OX. My position is latitude 58° 17.03′ S, longitude 039° 22.81 W - I repeat position: latitude 58° 17.03 S longitude 039° 22.81 W - I am aground full length. I am flooding below water line – I cannot control flooding for a long time. I require tug assistance and pumps. I have 184 persons on board. Warning: uncharted rocks in distress position.   OVER
Comment: Position (long) not correctly repeated

Task	MV Dundee/EJZD acknowledges this MAYDAY Position: 24 nm SW of distress position bearing: 225° speed: 22.8 kn; ETA: within 50 min

MAYDAY passenger vessel Morsh/R7OX this is Dundee/EJZD Received MAYDAY MAYDAY passenger liner Morsh (3x) R7OX this is Dundee (3x) call sign EJZD My position 24 nm SW of distress position- my speed to distress position 22.8 kn ETA at distress position within 50 minutes   OVER

All stations (3x)

this is Washington Hydrographical Office (3x)

with an information to shipping off Florida east coast.

Wreck light buoy No. 76 in position 28° 12′ N and 080° 29′ W

previously reported unlit has been relighted.

　OUT

SECURITE (3x)　　all ships (3x)　this is Osaka Radio (3x)

Advice: Listen to my safety message on VHF Ch. 13

　　OVER

SECURITE (3x)　all ships (3x)　　this is Osaka Radio (3x)

Typhoon warning of 222100 z.

Typhoon Dinah 265 mbs at 28° 50′ N and 129° 04′ E — West of

Mioshima Bay moving NE to NNE at 22 kn.

Maximum sustained winds 65 knots near centre. Winds of 40

knots within radius of 250 nm in eastern semicircle and within 100

nm in western semicircle.

No further information from Osaka Radio

　　OUT

Comment: Date/time group is not correctly spoken. Atmospheric
pressure is wrong.

PAN-PAN (3x)　ALL STATIONS　(3x)　　this is Kowloon Radio (3x)

Fishing vessel has lost Chinese male person aged 37 years in

position latitude 21°54′ North and 113° 40′ East.

Man is wearing light green rain coat.

All vessels in vicinity of mentioned position keep sharp look-out

and report any sightings to Hong Kong Maritime Department.

Date and time: 112000 Zulu.

　　OUT

SECURITE (3x)　　ALL STATIONS (3x)　　this is Cartagena Radio (3x)

Advice: Listen on VHF Ch. 73

　　OVER

SECURITE (3x)

ALL STATIONS (3x)

this is Cartagena Radio (3x)

Tropical storm warning at 1630 hours UTC.

Hurricane Lora with central pressure of 926 mbs located in position 11° 25′ North and 075° 30′ East.

Present movement NNE at 12 knots.

Winds of 55 to 60 kn within radius of 80 nm of centre.

Seas rough to high.

Further information on VHF Channel 68 at 18:00 hours UTC.

　　OUT

SECURITE (3x) all vessels in Junk Bay (3x)　this is Hong Kong Radio (3x)

Advice: Listen to the following safety message on VHF Ch. 11

　OVER

SECURITE (3x)

all vessels in Junk Bay (3x)

this is Hong Kong Radio (3x)

Gas escaping from drilling platform "Glomar Lantan" in position bearing 110 degrees, distance 1.3 nautical miles from Tseung Kwan.

Vessels are warned not to pass within a radius of 2000 m.

No further warnings for Junk Bay area.

　OUT

MAYDAY RELAY (3x)

ALL STATIONS (3x)

this is MT Tezikov (3x)/ LZAE

At 0534 hours UTC on 2182 kHz following received,

- begins:

Mayday

Dragon/HGTR.

My position 61° 10′ North and 003° 45′ East.

Heavily down by the stern due to flooding in the engine room.

I cannot stop the flooding.

I will abandon my vessel.

I require urgently assistance

- ends.

This is Tezikov / LZAE

　　OVER

SECURITE (3x)　　ALL STATIONS (3x)　　this is Anglosea (3x) / EALG

Advice: Listen to my safety message on VHF Ch. 11

　　OVER

SECURITE (3x)

ALL STATIONS (3x) this is Anglosea (3x) EALG

I have lost 31 20 foot empties in position latitude 18° 44.95′ North and longitude 061° 56.04′ East. Containers drifting to 055 degrees.

Warning: drifting containers danger to navigation

　　OUT

PAN-PAN (3x)   ALL STATIONS (3x)

this is Motor Tanker Russoneft (3x) SL4Q

Please listen to VHF Ch. 13.

 OVER

PAN-PAN (3x) ALL STATIONS (3x)

this is Motor Tanker Russoneft (3x) SL4Q

My position latitude 36° 54.89′ N longitude 023° 11.74′ E.

I am spilling big quantity of crude oil.

I require oil clearance assistance – danger of pollution.

Warning: Uncharted rocks in mentioned position

 OVER

MAYDAY (3x)   this is Tall ship Seagull (3X) AXQ9

Mayday Seagull / AXQ9

I have lost female cadet overboard in position 211 degrees 5.4

NM from Pemba Reef at 16:57 hours UTC. Cadet is in orange life

jacket. All ships please assist with search in vicinity of distress

position.

 OVER

8. INTRA-SHIP COMMUNICATION

(Ref.: annex IMO SMCP pp. 217~223)

8.1 Standard Wheel Orders

All wheel orders given should be repeated by the helmsman and the officer of the watch should ensure that they are carried out correctly and immediately. All wheel orders should be held until countermanded. The helmsman should report immediately if the vessel does not answer the wheel. When there is concern that the helmsman is inattentive s/he should be questioned:

"What is your heading ?" And s/he should respond:
"My heading is 125 degrees."

	Order	Meaning
1	*Midships*	Rudder to be held in the fore and aft position.
2	*Port / starboard five*	5° of port / starboard rudder to be held.
3	*Port / starboard ten*	10°of port / starboard rudder to be held.
4	*Port / starboard fifteen*	15°of port / starboard rudder to be held.
5	*Port / starboard twenty*	20°of port / starboard rudder to be held.
6	*Hard-a-port / starboard*	Rudder to be held fully over to port / starboard.
8	*Nothing to port/ starboard*	Avoid allowing the vessel's head to go to port / starboard
9	*Meet her*	Check the swing of the vessel's head, but not stop swing by putting on opposite rudder.
10	*Steady*	Reduce swing as rapidly as possible.

11 ***Ease to five / ten /***   Reduce amount of rudder to 5° / 10° / 15° /
    fifteen / twenty   20° and hold.

12 ***Steady as she goes***   Steer a steady course on the compass heading indicated at the time of the order. The helmsman is to repeat the order and call out the compass heading on receiving the order. When the vessel is steady on that heading, the helmsman is to call out: ***"Steady on 125, Sir"***

13 Keep the buoy A-3 on port side / starboard side.

14 Report if she does not answer the wheel.

15 Finished with wheel, no more steering.

When the officer of the watch requires a course to be steered by compass, the direction in which s/he wants the wheel turned should be stated followed by each numeral being said separately, including zero, for example:

Order Course to be steered

Port, steer one eight two	***182°***
Starboard, steer zero eight two	***082°***
steer three zero five	***305°***

On receipt of an order to steer, for example, 182°, the helmsman should repeat it and bring the vessel round steadily to the course ordered. When the vessel is steady on the course ordered, the helmsman is to call out:

"Steady on one eight two, Sir".

The person giving the order should acknowledge the helmsman's reply.

	우현 20°	10°로 줄임	125°에 정침
Order	*Stb'd 20 !*	*Ease to 10 !*	*Steady 125 !*
Repeat it	Stb'd 20	Ease to 10	Steady 125
DO SO	우현20도 전타후	우현 10°로	125도 정침 후
Call out/ Reply	*Stb'd 20, Sir!*	*Ease to 10, Sir!* *Stb'd 10, Sir!*	*125 Steady, Sir!*
Acknowledge	Thank you Roger, OK	Stb'd 10, OK Thank you	OK, Roger, 125 Thank you

8.2 Standard Engine Orders

Any engine order given should be repeated by the person operating the bridge telegraph(s) and the officer of the watch (OOW) should ensure the order is carried out correctly and immediately.

Order	Meaning
1. *Full ahead*	Engine power: full power ahead
2. *Half astern*	Engine power: half power astern
3. *Slow ahead*	Engine power: slow ahead
4. *Dead slow astern*	Engine power: very slow astern
5. *Stop engine*	
6. *Emergency full astern*	From full-ahead to full-astern
7. *Stand by engine*	ER personnel fully ready to manoeuver
8. *Finished with engine*	Operation of engines no longer required

In vessels fitted with twin propellers, the word "both" should be added to all orders affecting both shafts, e.g. "*Full ahead both*", and "*Slow astern both*", except that the words "*Stop all engines*" should be used, when appropriate. When required to manoeuver twin propellers independently, this should be indicated, i.e. "*Full ahead starboard*", "*Half astern port*", etc.

Where bow thrusters are used, the following orders are used:

9. *Bow thruster full to port.*
10. *Bow thruster half to starboard.*
11. *Bow thruster stop*

8.3 Pilot on the Bridge

8.3.1 Standard SMCP Phrases for manoeuvering

(Pilot) Is the engine a diesel or a turbine?
(OOW) The engine is a diesel.

(Pilot) Is the engine-room manned or is the engine on bridge control?
(OOW) The engine-room is manned. / The engine is on bridge control.

(Pilot) How long does it take to change the engines from ahead to astern?
(OOW) It takes 20 seconds to change the engines (from ahead to astern).

(Pilot) How long does it take to start the engines from stopped?
(OOW) It takes 13 seconds to start the engines (from stopped).

(Pilot) Do you have a single propeller or twin propellers?
(OOW) We have a single propeller.

(Pilot) Do you have a bow thruster or stern thruster?
(OOW) We have one bow thruster.

(Pilot) I require the pilot card / manoeuvering data.

(Pilot) How long does it take from hard-a-port to hard-a-starboard?
(OOW) It takes 20 seconds (from hard-a-port to hard-a-starboard).

(Pilot) Give 2 short blasts (on the whistle).
(Pilot) Maintain a speed of 10 knots.

(Pilot) Is the radar operational?
(OOW) Yes, the radar is operational.

(Pilot) Change the radar to 6 miles range scale.
(Pilot) Change the radar relative head-up / north-up / course-up.

(Pilot) What is your present maximum draft?

(OOW) My present maximum draft is 14 metres.

(Pilot) What is your air draft?

(OOW) My air draft is 42 metres.

8.3.2 Anchoring

We are going to anchorage.

We will let go port / starboard / both anchor(s).

We will let go port both anchor, Put 5 shackles in the water / on deck.

< Stand by Anchor 절차 및 Anchoring 관련 용어 >

(Capt) Stand by port anchor - (OOW) Repeat & Relay to Forecastle Deck - (C/O) S/B anchor 작업 지휘 - (C/O) 완료 후 선교에 보고 - (OOW) Acknowledge & report to Capt - (Capt) Acknowledge

Put windlass in gear.

Walk out the anchor.

Walk back port anchor one and half shackle in water.

Slack out the cable(s).
Check the cable(s).
Hold on the cable.
Switch on the anchor light. / Hoist the anchor ball.

Let go port / starboard / both anchor(s).

How is the cable leading?

The cable is leading :

~ ahead / astern. (12 O'clocks / 6 O'clocks)

~ to port / to starboard. (9 O'clocks / 3 O'clocks)

~ round the bow.

~ up and down.

How is the cable growing?

The cable is slack / tight / coming tight.

실무: *(C/O) Bridge / F'cle, 3 shackles in water, chain direction 10 O'clock, weak tension, Sir !* *(체인 길이, 체인방향, 장력 순서로 보고)*

Is the anchor holding?

Yes, the anchor is holding. / No, the anchor is not holding.

Is she brought up?

Yes, she is brought up[13]. / No, she is not brought up (yet).

Check the anchor position by bearings in every 20 minutes.

< Leaving the anchorage >

How much cables are out? / *5 shackles are out.*

How is the cable leading? / *The cable is leading ahead / astern, up & down:*

Heave up port cable. [Heave up (port) anchor.]

How much weight is on the cable?

Much / too much weight is on the cable.

No weight is on the cable.

Stop heaving.

How many shackles are left (to come in)?

3 shackles are left (to come in).

---

13 닻이 해저에 완전히 박혀서 발묘(拔錨)될 위험이 없으므로, 투묘작업을 완료해도 좋은 상태. *When the ship is settled down to her anchorage, is not dragging the anchor and has a steady strain on the cable.*

실무: *(C/O) Bridge / F'cle, 3 shackles on deck, Chain direction 10 O'clock, tight tension, Sir !* (체인 길이, 체인방향, 장력 순서로 보고)

The anchor is **aweigh**. (**Up & down anchor.**)

The anchor is clear of the water.

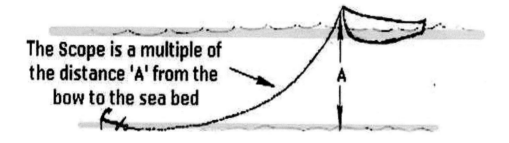

The Scope is a multiple of the distance 'A' from the bow to the sea bed

8.3.3 Tug assistance

We will take 2 tugs.

The tugs will meet you in position A-3 buoy at 14:00 hours.

The tugs will pull / push.

We use the towing lines of the tug. / of your vessel.

Stand by for making fast the tugs.

Send heaving line to the tugs.

Lower towing line to the tug.

Lower towing line 2 metres from the water.

Make fast the tugs.

Make fast one tug on port bow, another tug on port quarter.

Keep clear of towing line(s).

Stand by for letting go the tug(s).

Let go the tug(s).

8.4 Berthing and unberthing

Is the propeller clear?

   Yes, the propeller is clear.

Keep the propeller clear.

Have fenders ready fore and aft.

<Berthing>

We will berth port side / starboard side alongside.

We will moor

   ~ to buoy(s) (ahead and astern).

   ~ alongside.

   ~ to dolphins.

Send out

   ~ the head / stern / breast lines.

   ~ the forward / aft spring.

Do you have tension winches?

Yes, we have tension winches (forward and aft).

Have the heaving lines ready forward and aft.

Send the heaving / head / stern / breast line(s) ashore.

Pick up the slack on the head line.

Heave away. / Slack away.

Stop heaving.

Check the stern line.

Hold on the forward spring.

Heave in easy.

Keep the head line tight.

We have to move 30 metres ahead / astern.

We are in position.

Make fast fore and aft.

<Unberthing – Casting off>

Are you ready to get underway?
Yes, we are ready (to get underway).
We will be ready to get underway in 15 minutes.

Stand by for letting go.

Single up fore and aft.

Let go the head / stern line / the fore spring / aft spring

Let go all.

Finished with manoeuvering station.

Stand by starboard anchor.

< Excercise >

도선사가 "Is propeller clear?"라고 물었다. 이후의 통신내용을 순서에 따라 정리해 보기
•
•
•
•
•
•
•

도선사가 "How much cables are out How is the cable leading?"이라고 물었다.

이후의 통신내용을 순서에 따라 정리해 보기

-
-
-
-
-
-
-

Annex(1)

IMO STANDARD MARINE COMMUNICATION PHRASES

[IMO Res.A.918(22)]

CONTENTS

STANDARD MARINE COMMUNICATION PHRASES   PART A

PART A covers Phrases applicable in external communications from ship to shore, shore to ship and ship to ship as required by STCW 1978, as revised, Table A-II/1, as well as Phrases applicable on board vessels in conversations between Pilots and bridge teams as required by Regulation 14(4) of Chapter V of SOLAS 1974, as revised.

AI   EXTERNAL COMMUNICATION PHRASES

Attention: The use of Standard Phrases in vessels' external communication does not in any way exempt from applying the radiotelephone procedures as set out in the ITU Radio Regulations.

AI/1   Distress traffic

The distress traffic controlling station/other stations may impose radio silence on any interfering stations by using the term:
Seelonce Mayday / Distress"
unless the latter have messages about the distress.

AI/1.1   Distress communications

Note: A distress traffic has always to commence with stating the position of the vessel in distress as specified in "GENERAL 11 Positions / 13 Bearings" if it is not included in the DSC distress alert.

.1   **Fire, explosion**

.1   I am / MV ... on fire (- after explosion).
.2   Where is the fire?
  .2.1   Fire is
      ~ on deck.
      ~ in engine-room.
      ~ in hold(s).
      ~ in superstructure / accommodation / ... .
.3   Are dangerous goods on fire?
  .3.1   Yes, dangerous goods are on fire.
  .3.2   No, dangerous goods are not on fire.
.4   Is there danger of explosion?

.4.1　Yes,　danger of explosion.

.4.2　No danger of explosion.

.5　　I am / MV　... not under command.

.6　　Is the fire under control?

.6.1　Yes, fire is under control.

.6.2　No, fire is not under control.

.7　　What kind of assistance is required?

.7.1　I do not / MV ... does not require assistance.

.7.2　I require / MV ... requires

　　　　~ fire fighting assistance.

　　　　~ breathing apparatus - smoke is toxic.

　　　　~ foam extinguishers / CO_2 extinguishers.

　　　　~ fire pumps.

　　　　~ medical assistance / ... .

.8　　Report injured persons.

.8.1　No persons injured.

.8.2　Number of injured persons / casualties: ... .

.2　**Flooding**

.1　　I am/ MV ... is flooding below water line.

.2　　I / MV ... cannot control flooding.

.3　　What kind of assistance is required?

.3.1　I require / MV ... requires pumps / divers, ...

.3.2　I will send pumps / divers / ... .

.3.3　I cannot send pumps / divers ... .

.4　　I have / MV ... has dangerous list to port side / starboard.

.5　　I am / MV ... in critical condition.

.6　　Flooding is under control.

.7　　I / MV ... can proceed without assistance.

.8　　I require / MV ... requires escort / tug assistance /... .

.3　**Collision**

.1　　I have / MV ... has collided

　　　　~ with MV... .

    ~ with unknown vessel / object / ... .

    ~ with ...(name) light vessel.

    ~ with seamark ... (charted name).

    ~ with iceberg / ... .

.2 Report damage.

  .2.1 I have / MV .. has damage above / below water line.

  .2.2 I am / MV ... not under command.

.3 I / MV cannot repair damage.

.4 I / MV ... can only proceed at slow speed.

.5 What kind of assistance is required?

  .5.1 I require / MV ... requires / escort / tug assistance /... .

.4 Grounding

.1 I am / MV ... aground.

.2 I require / MV ... requires tug assistance / pumps / ... .

.3 What part of your vessel is aground?

  .3.1 Aground forward / amidships /aft / full length.

.4 Warning. Uncharted rocks in position ... .

.5 Risk of grounding at low water.

.6 I / MV ... will jettison cargo to refloat.

  .6.1 Warning! Do not jettison IMO-Class cargo!

.7 When do you / does MV ...   expect to refloat?

  .7.1 I expect / MV ... expects to refloat

     ~ at ... UTC.

     ~ when tide rises.

     ~ when weather improves.

     ~ when draft decreases.

     ~ with tug assistance / ... .

.8 Can you / can MV ... beach?

  .8.1 I / MV ... can / will beach in position ... .

  .8.2 I / MV ... cannot beach.

.5 List - danger of capsizing

.1 I have / MV ... has dangerous list to port / starboard.

.2   I / MV ... will

        ~ transfer cargo / bunkers to stop listing.

        ~ jettison cargo to stop listing.

.3   I am / MV ... in danger of capsizing (- list increasing).

.6   Sinking

.1   I am / MV ... sinking after collision / grounding / flooding / explosion / ...

.2   I require / MV ... requires assistance.

.3   I am / MV ... proceeding to your assistance.

.4   ETA at distress position within ... hours / at ... UTC.

.7   **Disabled and adrift**

.1   I am / MV ...

        ~ not under command.

        ~ adrift.

        ~ drifting at ... knots to ... (cardinal points).

.2   I require / MV ... requires tug assistance.

.8   **Armed attack / piracy**

.1   I am / MV ... under attack by pirates.

    .1.1   I / MV ... was under attack by pirates.

.2   I require / MV ... requires assistance.

.3   What kind of assistance is required?

    .3.1   I require / MV ... requires

        ~ medical assistance.

        ~ navigational assistance.

        ~ military assistance.

        ~ tug assistance.

        ~ escort / ... .

.4   Report damage.

    .4.1   I have / MV .. has

        ~ no damage.

~ damage to navigational equipment / ... .

.4.2   I am / MV ... not under command.

.5   Can you / can MV ... proceed?

.5.1   Yes, I / MV ... can proceed.

.5.2 No, I / MV ... cannot proceed.

.9   **Undesignated distress**

.1   I have /   MV ... has problems with cargo / engine(s) / navigation / ... .

.2   I require / MV ... requires ... .

.10   **Abandoning vessel**

.1   I / crew of MV ... must abandon vessel ... after explosion / collision /grounding / flooding / piracy / armed attack / ... .

.11   **Person overboard**

.1   I have / MV ... has lost person overboard in position ... .

.2   Assist with search in vicinity of position ... .

.3   All vessels in vicinity of position ... keep sharp lookout and report to ...

.4   I am / MV.. is proceeding for assistance - ETA at ... UTC / within ... hours.

.5   Search in vicinity of position ... .

.5.1   I am / MV ... is searching in vicinity of position ... .

.6   Aircraft ETA at ... UTC / within ... hours to assist in search.

.7   Can you continue search?

.7.1   Yes, I can continue search.

.7.2   No, I cannot continue search.

.8   Stop search.

.8.1   Return to ... .

.8.2   Proceed with your voyage.

.10 What is the result of search?

.10.1   The result of search is negative.

.11   I / MV ... located / picked up person(s) in position ... .

.12   Person picked up is crewmember / passenger of MV ... .

.13   What is condition of person(s)?

    .13.1   Condition of person(s) bad / good.

    .13.2   Person(s) dead.

AI/1.2   Search and Rescue communication

.1   **SAR communications (specifying or supplementary to 1.1)**

.1   I require / MV ... requires assistance.

.2   I am / MV ... proceeding to your assistance.

.3   What is your MMSI number?

    .3.1   My MMSI number is .... .

.4   What is your position?

    .4.1   My position ... .

.5   What is your present course and speed?

    .5.1   My present course ... degrees, my speed   ...   knots.

.6   Report number of persons on board?

    .6.1   Number of persons on board: ... .

.7   Report injured persons.

    .7.1   No person injured

    .7.2   Number of injured persons / casualties: ... .

.8   Will you abandon vessel?

    .8.1   I will not abandon vessel.

    .8.2   I will abandon vessel at ... UTC.

.9   Is your EPIRB switched on?

    .9.1   Yes, my EPIRB is switched on/inadvertently switched on.

.10   Did you transmit a DSC distress alert?

    .10.1   Yes, I did transmit.

    .10.2   No, I inadvertently transmitted.

.11   How many lifeboats / liferafts (with how many persons) will you launch?

    .11.1   I will launch ... lifeboats / liferafts (with ... persons).

.12   How many persons will stay on board?

.12.1 No person will stay on board.

.12.2 ... persons will stay on board.

.13 What is the weather situation in your position?

.13.1 Wind ...(cardinal points) force Beaufort ... .

.13.2 Visibility good/moderate/poor.

.13.3 Smooth/moderate/rough/high Sea / slight/moderate/heavy swell ...(cardinal points).

.13.4 Current ... knots, to ...(cardinal points).

.14 Are there dangers to navigation?

.14.1 No dangers to navigation.

.14.2 Warning! Uncharted rocks / ice / abnormally low tides. mines / ...

.2 **Acknowledgement and / or relay of SAR messages**

.1 Received MAYDAY from MV ... at UTC on VHF Channel ... / frequency ....

.2 Vessel in position ...

~ on fire

~ had explosion.

~ flooded.

~ in collision (with ..).

~ listing / in danger of capsizing.

~ sinking.

~ disabled and adrift.

~ abandoned / ... .

.3 Vessel requires assistance.

.4 Received your MAYDAY.

.4.1 My position ... .

.4.2 I / MV ... will proceed to your assistance.

.4.3 ETA at distress position within ... hours / at ... UTC.

.3 **Performing / coordinating SAR operations**

The questions are normally asked and advice is given by the On-scene Coordinator (OSC).

For further information see IAMSAR Manual, London/ Montreal, 1998.

.1   I will act as On-scene Coordinator.

    .1.1   I will show following signals / lights: ... .

.2   Can you proceed to distress position?

    .2.1   Yes, I can proceed to distress position.

    .2.2   No, I cannot proceed to distress position.

.3   What is your ETA at distress position?

    .3.1   My ETA at distress position within ... hours / at ... UTC.

.4   MAYDAY position is not correct.

    .4.1   Correct MAYDAY position is ... .

.5   Vessels are advised to proceed to position ... to start rescue.

.6   Carry out search pattern ... starting at ... UTC.

.7   Initial course ... degrees, search speed ... knots.

.8   Carry out radar search.

.9   MV ... allocated track number ... .

.10   MV / MVs ... adjust interval between vessels to ...kilometres / nautical miles.

.11   Adjust track spacing to ...kilometres / nautical miles.

.12   Search speed now ... knots.

.13   Alter course

      ~ to ... degrees (- at ... UTC).

      ~ for next leg of track now / at ... UTC.

.14   We resume search in position ... .

.15   Crew has abandoned vessel / MV ... .

.16   Keep sharp lookout for lifeboats / liferafts / persons in water / ... .

.4   **Finishing with SAR operations**

.1   What is the result of search?

    .1.1   The result of search is negative.

.2   Sighted

      ~ vessel in position ... .

      ~ lifeboats / life rafts in position ... .

      ~ persons in water / ... in position ... .

.3   Continue search in position ... .

.4   Can you pick up survivors?

    .4.1   Yes, I can pick up survivors.

    .4.2   No, I cannot pick up survivors.

.5   MV ... / I will proceed to pick up survivors.

    .5.1   Stand by lifeboats / liferafts.

.6   Picked up

        ~   ... survivors in position ... .

        ~   ... lifeboats / liferafts (with ... persons / casualties) in position ... .

        ~   ... persons / casualties in lifejackets in position ... .

        ~   ... in position ... .

.7   Survivors in bad / good condition.

.8   Do you require medical assistance?

    .8.1   Yes, I require medical assistance.

    .8.2   No, I do not require medical assistance.

.9   Try to obtain information from survivors.

.10   There are

        ~ still ... lifeboats / liferafts with survivors.

        ~ no more lifeboats / liferafts.

.11   Total number of persons on board was ... .

.12   All persons / ... persons rescued.

.13   You / MV ... may stop search and proceed with voyage.

.14   There is no hope to rescue more persons.

.15   We finish with SAR operations.

AI/1.3 Requesting medical assistance

.1   I require / MV ... requires medical assistance.

.2   What kind of assistance is required?

    .2.1   I require / MV ... requires

        ~ boat for hospital transfer.

        ~ radio medical advice.

        ~ helicopter with doctor (to pick up person(s)).

.3   I / MV ... will

        ~ send boat.

      ~ send helicopter with doctor

      ~ send helicopter to pick up person(s).

      ~ arrange for radio medical advice on VHF Channel ... / frequency ... .

.4   Boat / helicopter ETA at ... UTC / within ... hours.

.5   Do you have doctor on board?

   .5.1   Yes, I have doctor on board.

   .5.2   No, I have no doctor on board.

.6   Can you make rendezvous in position ... ?

   .6.1   Yes, I can make rendezvous in position at ... UTC / within ... hours.

.6.2   No, I cannot make rendezvous.

.7   I / MV ... will send boat / helicopter to transfer doctor.

.8   Transfer person(s) to my vessel / to MV ... by boat / helicopter.

.9   Transfer of person(s) not possible.

AI/2 Urgency traffic

Safety of a vessel (other than distress).

Note: An urgency traffic has always to commence with stating the position of the calling vessel if it is not included in the DSC alert.

.1   Technical failure

.1   I am / MV ... not under command.

.2   What problems do you have / does MV ... have?

   .2.1   I have / MV ... has problems with engine(s) / steering gear / propelle / ... .

.3   I am / MV ...is manoeuvering with difficulty.

.4   Keep clear of me / MV ... .

.5   Navigate with caution.

.6   I require / MV ... requires tug assistance / escort / ... .

.7   I try / MV ... tries to proceed without assistance.

.8   Stand by on VHF Channel ... / frequency ... .

   .8.1   Standing by on VHF Channel ... / frequency ... .

.2   **Cargo**

.1   I have / MV has ... lost dangerous goods of IMO Class ... in position ... .

.2   Containers / barrels / drums / bags / ... with dangerous goods of IMO Class ... adrift near position ... .

.3   I am / MV ... is spilling

~ dangerous goods of IMO Class ... in position ...

~ crude oil / ... in position ... .

.4   I require / MV... requires oil clearance assistance danger of pollution.

.5   I am / MV ... is dangerous source of radiation.

.3   **Ice damage**

.1   I have / MV ... has damage above / below waterline.

.2   What kind of assistance is required?

.2.1   I require / MV ... requires

~ tug assistance.

~ icebreaker assistance / escort / ... .

.3   I have / MV ... has stability problems - heavy icing.

.4   Can you proceed without assistance?

.4.1   Yes, I can proceed without assistance.

.4.2   No, I cannot proceed without assistance.

.5   Stand by on VHF Channel ... / frequency ... .

.5.1   Standing by on VHF Channel ... / frequency ... .

AI/3   Safety Communications

AI/3.1   Meteorological and hydrological conditions

.1   **Winds, storms, tropical storms, sea state**

.1   What is wind direction and force in your position / in position ... ?

.1.1   Wind direction ...(cardinal points), force Beaufort ... in my position / in position ... .

.2   What wind is expected in my position / in position ... ?

.2.1 The wind in your position / in position ... is expected

~ from direction... (cardinal points), force Beaufort ... .

~ to increase / decrease.

~ variable.

.3 What is the latest gale / storm warning?

.3.1 The latest gale / storm warning is as follows: Gale / storm warning. Winds at ... UTC in area ... (met.area) from direction ...(cardinal points) and force Beaufort ... backing / veering to ... (cardinal points).

.4 What is the latest tropical storm warning?

.4.1 The latest tropical storm warning is as follows: Tropical storm warning at ... TC. Hurricane... (name) / tropical cyclone / tornado/ willywilly / typhoon ... (name) with central pressure of ... millibars / hPascals located in position ... Present movement... (cardinal points) at ... knots. Winds of ... knots within radius of ... miles of centre. Seas smooth / moderate / rough/high. Further information on VHF Channel ... / frequency ... .

.5 What is the atmospheric pressure in your position / in position ... ?

.5.1 The atmospheric pressure in your position / in position ... is ... millibars/hPascals.

.6 What is the barometric Change in your position / in position ... ?

.6.1 The barometric Change in your position / in position ... is ... millibars / hPascals per hour / within the last ... hours.

.6.2 The barometer is steady / dropping (rapidly) / rising (rapidly).

.7 What maximum winds are expected in the storm area?

.7.1 Maximum winds of ... knots are expected

~ in the storm area.

~ within a radius of ... kilometres / miles of the centre.

~ in the safe / dangerous semicircle.

.8 What is sea state in your position / in position ... ?

.8.1 The smooth / moderate / rough / high sea/ slight / moderate / heavy swell in my position / in position ... is ... metres from... (cardinal points).

.9 Is the sea state expected to change (- within the next

hours)?

.9.1   No, the sea state is not expected to change (- within the next hours).

.9.2   Yes, a sea / swell of ... metres from ...(cardinal points) is expected (- within the next hours).

.10   A tsunami / an abnormal wave is expected by ... UTC.

.2   **Restricted visibility**

.1   What is visibility in your position / in position ... ?

.1.1   Visibility in my position / in position is ... metres / nautical miles

.1.2   Visibility is restricted by mist / fog / snow / dust / rain.

.1.3   Visibility is increasing / decreasing / variable.

.2   Is visibility expected to change in my position / in position ... (within the next hours)?

.2.1   No, visibility is not expected to change in your position / in position... (- within the next hours).

.2.2   Yes, visibility is expected to increase / decrease to ... metres / nautical miles in your position / in position ... (within the next hours).

.2.3   Visibility is expected to be variable between ... metres / nautical miles in your position / in position ... (within the next hours).

.3   **Ice**

.1   What is the latest ice information?

.1.1   Ice warning. Ice / iceberg(s) located in position ... / reported in area around ...

.1.2   No ice located in position ... / reported in area around ... .

.2   What ice situation is expected in my position / area around ... ?

.2.1   Ice situation is

~   not expected to change in your position / area around ... .

~ expected to improve / deteriorate in your position / area around ... .

.2.2　Thickness of ice is expected to increase / decrease in your position / area around ... .

.3　Navigation is dangerous in area around ... due to floating ice / pack ice / iceberg(s).

.4　Navigation in area around ... is only possible

~ for highpowered vessels of strong construction .

~ with ice-breaker assistance.

.5　Area around ...　temporarily closed for navigation.

.6　Danger of icing in area around ... .

.4　**Abnormal tides**

.1　The present　tide　... is metres above / below datum in position ... .

.2　The tide ... is metres above/below prediction.

.3　The tide is rising / falling.

.4　Wait until high / low water.

.5　Abnormally high / low tides are expected in position ... at about ... UTC / within ... hours.

.6　Is the depth of water sufficient in position ... ?

.6.1　Yes, the depth of water is sufficient in position ... .

.6.2　No, the depth of water is not sufficient in position ... .

.6.3　The depth of water is ... metres in position ... .

.7　My draft ... is metres - can I enter / pass ... (charted name of place)?

.7.1　Yes, you can enter / pass (charted name of place).

.7.2　No, you cannot enter / pass (charted name of place) - wait until ... UTC.

.8　The charted depth of water is increased / decreased by ... metres due to sea state / winds.

AI/3.2　Navigational warnings involving

.1　**Land- or seamarks**

Defects

.1　...(charted name of light / buoy) in position ...

~ unlit / unreliable / damaged / destroyed / off station / missing.

Alterations

.2   ... (charted name of lightbuoy / buoy) in position ...

~   (temporarily) changed to ...(full characteristics).

~ (temporarily) removed.

~ (temporarily) discontinued.

New and moved

.3   ...(charted name of light / buoy) ...(full characteristics)

~ established in position ... .

~   re-established in position ... .

~ moved ... kilometres / nautical miles in ... (direction) to position ... .

.4   (Note: Only for major fog signal stations.)

Fog signal ...(charted name of light / buoy) in position ... inoperative.

.2   **Drifting objects**

.1   Superbuoy / mine / unlit derelict vessel / ... (number) container(s) adrift in vicinity ...(position) at ...(date and time if known).

.3   **Electronic navigational aids**

.1   GPS Satellite ...(number) unusable from ... (date and time) to ...(date and time). ancel one hour after time of restoration.

.2   LORAN station ...(name or number of master / secondary) off air from ...(date and time) to ... (date and time). Cancel one hour after time of restoration.

.3   RACON ... (name of station) in position ... off air from ...(date and time) to... (date and time). Cancel one hour after time of restoration.

.4   **Seabottom characteristics, wrecks**

Use REPORTED when position is unconfirmed, and use LOCATED when position has been confirmed by survey or other means

.1   Uncharted reef / rock / shoal / dangerous wreck / obstruction reported / located in position ... .

.2   Dangerous wreck in position ... marked by ... (type)buoy ... (distance in kilometres / nautical miles) ... (direction).

.5   Miscellaneous

.5.1   Cable, pipeline and seismic / hydrographic operations

.1   Cable / pipeline operations by ... (vessel) in vicinity / along line joining ... (positions) from ...(date and time)to ...(date and time). Wide berth requested (if requested). Contact via VHF channel ... (if requested).

.2   Seismic survey / hydrographic operations by ... (vessel) from ... (date and time) to... (date and time) in ... (position). Wide berth requested. (if requested). Contact via VHF Channel ... (if requested).

.3   Survey vessel ...(name) towing ... (length) seismic cable along line joining / in area bounded by / in vicinity ...(position) from ...(date and time) to ... (date and time). Wide berth requested (if requested). Contact via VHF Channel ... (if requested).

.4   Hazardous operations by ...(vessel) in area bounded by / in vicinity ... (position) from ... (date and time) to ... (date and time). Wide berth requested (if requested). Contact via VHF Ch .... (if requested).

.5   Current meters / hydrographic instruments moored in ... (position). Wide berth requested (if requested).

.5.2   Diving, towing and dredging operations

.1   Diving / dredging operations by vessel ... (name) from ...(date and time) to ...(date and time) in position ... . Wide berth requested (if requested).

.2   Difficult tow from ... (port of departure)on ... (date) to ... (destination) on ... (date). Wide berth requested.

.5.3   Tanker transhipment

.1   Transhipment of ... (kind of cargo) in position ... . Wide berth requested.

.2   I am / MT ... spilling oil / chemicals / ... in position....Wide berth requested.

.3   I am / LNG-tanker ... leaking gas in position ... - do not pass to windward.

.4   Oil clearance operations near MT ... in position ... . Wide berth requested.

.5.4   Off-shore installations, rig moves

.1   Platform ... (name/number if available) reported / established in position ... at ... (date and time). Wide berth requested (if requested).

.2   Platform ... (name/number if available) removed from ... (position) on ... (date).

.3   Pipeline / platform ... (name/number if available) in position ... spilling oil / leaking gas. Wide berth requested.

.4   Derelict platform ... (name / number if available) being removed from ... (position) at ... (date and time). Wide berth requested.

.5.5   Defective locks or bridges

.1   Lock ... (name) defective.

.1.1   For entering ... (charted name of place) use lock ... (name).

.2   Lock / bridge ... (name) defective.

.2.1   Avoid this area - no possibility for vessels to turn.

.5.6   Military operations

.1   Gunnery / rocket firing / missile / torpedo / underwater ordnance exercises in area bounded by ... (positions) from ... (date and time) to ... (date and time). Wide berth requested (if requested).

.2   Mine clearing operations from ... (date time) to ... (date and time) in area bounded by ... (positions). Wide berth requested. Contact via VHF channel ... (number) (if requested).

.5.7 Fishery

.1 Small fishing boats in area around ... - navigate with caution.

.2 Is fishing gear ahead of me?

   .2.1 No fishing gear ahead of you.

   .2.2 Yes, fishing gear with buoys / without buoys in position ... / area around ... - navigate with caution.

.3 Fishing gear has fouled my propeller(s).

.4 You have caught my fishing gear.

.5 Advise you to recover your fishing gear.

.6 Fishing in area ... prohibited.

AI/3.3 Environmental protection communications

.1 Located oil spill in position ... extending ... (length and width in metres) to ... (cardinal points).

.2 Located oil spill

   ~ in your wake.

   ~ in the wake of MV ... .

.3 I have / MV ... has accidental spillage of oil / ... .

.4 Can you / MV ... stop spillage?

   .4.1 Yes, I / MV ... can stop spillage.

   .4.2 No, I / MV ... cannot stop spillage.

.5 What kind of assistance is required?

   .5.1 I require / MV ... requires

      - oil clearance assistance.

      - floating booms / oil dispersants / ... .

.5 Stay in vicinity of pollution and cooperate with oil clearance team.

.6 ... (number) barrels / drums / containers with IMDG Code marks reported adrift near position ..... .

.7 Located a vessel dumping chemicals / waste / ... in position ... .

   .7.1 Located a vessel incinerating chemicals / waste / ... in position ...

.8 Can you identify the polluter?

   .8.1 Yes, I can identify the polluter - polluter is MV ... .

.8.2   No, I cannot identify the polluter.
.9   What is course and speed of the polluter?
  .9.1   Course of the polluter ... degrees, speed ... knots.
  .9.2   The polluter left the scene.

AI/4   Pilotage

AI/4.1   Pilot request
See AI / 6 - .4.3 "Pilot request"

AI/4.2   Embarking / disembarking pilot

.1   Stand by pilot ladder.
.2   Rig the pilot ladder on port side / starboard side ... metres above   water.
.3   The pilot ladder is   rigged on port side / starboard side.
.4   You must rig another pilot ladder
.5   The pilot ladder is unsafe.
.6   What is wrong with the pilot ladder?
.7.   The pilot ladder
            ~ has broken / loose steps.
            ~ has broken spreaders.
            ~ has spreaders too short.
            ~ is too far aft / forward.
.8   Move the pilot ladder
            ~ ... metres aft / forward.
            ~ clear of discharge.
.9   Rig the accommodation ladder in combination with the pilot ladder.
.10   Rig the pilot ladder alongside hoist.
.11   Put lights on at the pilot ladder.
.12   Man ropes are   required / not required.
.13   Have a heaving line ready at the pilot ladder.
.14   Correct the list of the vessel.
.15   Make a lee on your port side / starboard side.
.16   Steer ... degrees to make a lee.

.17   Keep the sea on your port quarter / starboard quarter.

.18   Make a boarding speed of ... knots.

.19   Stop engine(s) until pilot boat is clear.

.20   Put helm hard to port / starboard.

.21   Alter course to ... (cardinal points) - the pilot boat cannot clear the vessel.

.22   Put engine(s) ahead / astern.

.23   Embarkation is not possible.

     .23.1   Boarding arrangements do not comply with SOLAS Regulations.

     .23.2   Vessel is not suited for the pilot ladder.

AI/4.3   Tug request

.1   Must I take tug(s)?

     .1.1   Yes, you must take ... tug(s).

     .1.2   No, you need not take tug(s).

.2   How many tugs must I take?

     .2.1   You must take ... tug(s) according to Port Regulations.

     .2.2   You must take ... tug(s) fore and ... tug(s) aft.

.3   I require ... tug(s).

.4   In what position will the tug(s) meet me?

     .4.1   The tug(s) will meet you in position ... at ...UTC.

     .4.2   Wait for the tug(s) in position ... .

.5   Must I use the towing lines of my vessel?

     .5.1   Yes, you must use the towing lines.

     .5.2   No, you must use the towing lines of the tug.

AI/5   Specials

AI/5.1   Helicopter operations

     (H: = from helicopter   V: = from vessel)

.1   V: I require a helicopter.

        ~ to pick up persons.

        ~ with doctor.

~ with liferaft / ... .

.1.1   MRCC: I will send a helicopter with ... .

.2   H: MV ..., I will drop ... .

.3   H: MV ..., are you ready for the helicopter?

   .3.1   V: Yes, I am ready for the helicopter.

   .3.2   V: No, I am not ready for the helicopter (yet).

   .3.3   V: Ready for the helicopter in ... minutes.

.4   H: MV ... , helicopter is on the way to you.

.5   H: MV ... , what is your position.

   .5.1   V: My position is ... .

.6   H: MV ... , what is your present course and speed.

   .6.1   V: My present course is ... degrees, speed is ... knots.

.7   H: MV ... , make identification signals.

.8   V: I am making identification signals by smoke (buoy) / search light / flags / signalling lamp / ... .

.9   H: MV ..., you are identified.

.10   H: MV ..., what is the relative wind direction in degrees and knots.

   .10.1   V: The relative wind direction is ... degrees and ... knots.

.11   H: MV ..., keep the wind on port / starboard bow.

.12   H: MV ..., keep the wind on port / starboard quarter.

.13   H: MV ..., indicate the landing / pick-up area.

   .13.1   V: The landing / pick-up area is ... .

.14   H: MV ..., can I land on deck?

   .14.1   V: Yes, you can land on deck.

   .14.2   V: No, you cannot land on deck (yet).

   .14.3   V: You can land on deck in ... minutes.

.15   H: MV ..., I will use hoist / rescue sling / rescue basket / rescue net rescue litter / rescue seat / double lift.

.16   V: I am ready to receive you.

.17   H: MV ..., I am landing.

.18   H: MV ..., I am starting operation.

.19   H: MV ..., do not fix the hoist cable.

.20   H: MV ..., operation finished.

.21   H: MV ..., I am taking off.

AI/5.2 Ice breaker operations

.1 Ice breaker request

.1 I am / MV is ... fast in ice in position ... .

.2 I require / MV ... requires icebreaker assistance to reach ... .

.3 Icebreaker assistance

~ will arrive at ... UTC / within ... hours.

~ is not available until ... UTC.

~ is available only up to latitude... longitude ....

~ is suspended until ... (date and time).

~ is suspended after sunset.

~ is suspended until favourable weather conditions.

~ will be resumed at ... UTC.

.2 Ice breaker assistance for convoy

Icebreaker commands applying to all the vessels in a convoy have to be immediately confirmed consecutively by each vessel in turn and executed according to the pattern given in GENERAL 4.6. Icebreaker commands applying to a single vessel are confirmed and executed only by that vessel, this applies also for close coupled towing. When being assisted by an ice-breaker it is important to maintain a continuous listening watch on the appropriate VHF Channel and to maintain a proper lookout for sound and visual signals.

.1 Ice breaker assistance for convoy will start now / at ... UTC.

.2 Your place in convoy is number ... .

.3 MV ... will follow you.

.4 You will follow MV ... .

.5 Go ahead and follow me.

.5.1 Do not follow me.

.6 Proceed along the ice channel.

.7 Increase / reduce your speed.

.8 Reverse your engines.

.9 Stop engines.

.10   Keep a distance of ... metres /cables between vessels.

.11   Increase / reduce the distance between vessels to ... metres / cables.

.12   Stand by for receiving towing line.

   .12.1   Stand by for letting go towing line.

.13   Switch on the bow / stern search light

.14   Stop in present position.

.15   Icebreaker ... will escort you.

.16   Icebreaker assistance for convoy finished.

   .16.1   Open water / light ice conditions ahead.

.17   Proceed by yourself (to area ...).

.3   **Ice   breaker assistance in close-coupled towing**

.1   Stand by for close coupled towing.

.2   Slack out your anchors under the hawsepipes.

.3   Pass heaving lines through the hawsepipes.

.4   Receive towing line on deck.

.5   Lash together the eyes of the towing line with manila lashing.

.6   Fasten towing line on your bitts.

.7   I start to draw your bow into the stern notch of the icebreaker.

.8   Stand by for cutting the manila lashing if required.

.9   Keep yourself in the centreplane of the icebreaker.

AI/6   Vessel Traffic Service (VTS) Standard Phrases

AI/6.1   Phrases for acquiring and providing data for a traffic image

.1   **Acquiring and providing routine traffic data**

.1   What is the name of your vessel and call sign / identification?

   .1.1   The name of my vessel is ... , call sign ... / identification ... .

   .1.2   Spell the name of your vessel.

.2   What is your flag state?

   .2.1   My flag state is ... .

.3   What is your position?

   .3.1   My position is ... .

.4   What is your present course and speed?

   .4.1   My present course is ... degrees, my speed is ... knots.

.5   From what direction are you approaching?

   .5.1   I am approaching from ... .

.6   What is your port of destination / destination?

   .6.1   My port of destination / destination is ... .

.7   What was your last port of call?

   .7.1   My last port of call was ... .

.8   What is your ETA in position ... ?

   .8.1   My ETA is ...   UTC.

.9   What is your ETD from ... ?

   .9.1   My ETD from ... is ...   UTC.

.10   What is your draft forward / aft?

   .10.1   My draft forward / aft is ... metres.

.11   What is your present maximum draft ?

   .11.1   My present maximum draft is ... metres.

.12   What is your freeboard?

   .12.1   My freeboard is ... metres.

.13   What is your air draft?

   .13.1   My air draft is ... metres.

.14   Are you underway?

   .14.1   Yes, I am underway.

   .14.2   No, I am not underway.

   .14.3   I am ready to get underway.

.15   What is your full speed / full manoeuvering speed?

   .15.1   My full speed / full manoeuvering speed is ... knots.

.16   What is your cargo?

   .16.1   My cargo is ... .

.17   Do you carry any dangerous goods?

   .17.1   Yes, I carry the following dangerous goods: ... kilogrammes / tonnes IMO Class ... .

   .17.2   No, I do not carry any dangerous goods.

.18   Do you have any deficiencies / restrictions?

    .18.1   No, I have no deficiencies / restrictions.

    .18.2   Yes, I have the following deficiencies / restrictions: ... .

.19   I am / MV ... is constrained by draft.

.20   The maximum permitted draft is   ... metres.

.21   Do you have any list?

.21.1   Yes, I have a list to port / starboard of ... degrees.

    .21.2   No, I have no list.

.22   Are you on even keel?

    .22.1   Yes, I am on even keel.

    .22.2   No, I am trimmed by the head / stern.

.2   **Acquiring and providing distress traffic data**
    See AI/1.1 "Distress communications "

AI/6.2 Phrases for providing VTS services

.1   **Information service**
These phrases are normally transmitted from the shore.

.1.1   **Navigational warnings**

.1   Unknown object(s) in position ... .

.2   Ice / iceberg(s) in position ... / area around ... .

.3   Unlit derelict vessel adrift in vicinity ... at ... (date and time).

.4   Dangerous wreck / obstruction located in position ... marked by ... (type) buoy.

.5   Hazardous mine adrift in vicinity ... at ... (date and time).

.6   Uncharted reef / rock / shoal reported in position ... .

.7   Pipeline is leaking gas / oil in position ... - wide berth requested.

.8   Depth of water not sufficient in position ... .

.9   Navigation closed in area ... .

.1.2   **Navigational information**

.1   Oil spill in position ... .

.2   Current meters / hydrographic instruments moored in position ... - wide berth requested.

.3   Platform ...(name / number) reported / established in position ... - wide berth requested.

.4   ...(Charted name of light / buoy) in position ...

       ~ unlit / unreliable / damaged / destroyed / off station / missing.

          ~ (temporarily) changed to ...(full characteristics).

          ~ (temporarily) removed.

          ~ (temporarily) discontinued.

.5   ...(charted name of light / buoy) ...(full characteristics)

          ~ established in position ... .

          ~ re-established in position ... .

          ~ moved ... kilometres / nautical miles in ... (direction) to position ... .

.6   (Note: Only for major fog signal stations.)

       Fog signal ...(charted name of light / buoy) in position ... inoperative.

.1.3   Traffic information

.1   Gunnery / rocket firing / missile / torpedo / underwater ordnance exercises in area bounded by ...(positions) and ... from ... (date and time) to ... (date and time). Wide berth requested.

.2   Cable / pipeline operations by ... (vessel) in vicinity ... / along a line joining ... (position) from ... (date and time) to... (date and time) - wide berth requested. Contact via VHF channel ...

.3   Salvage operations in position ... from ... (date and time) to ... (date and time) - wide berth requested. Contact via VHF channel ... .

.4   Seismic / hydrographic operations by ... (vessel)... from ... (date and time) to ...(date and time) in position ... - wide berth requested. Contact via VHF Channel ... .

.5   Oil clearance operations near MT ... in position ... - wide berth requested.

.6   Transhipment of ... (kind of cargo) in position ... - wide berth requested.

.7   Difficult tow from ...(port of departure) to ... (destination) on ...(date)- wide berth requested.

.8   Vessel not under command in position ... / area ... .

.9   Hampered vessel in position ... area ... (course ... degrees, speed ... knots).

.10   Vessel in position ... on course ... and speed ... is not complying with traffic regulations.

.11   Vessel is crossing ... traffic lane on course ... and speed ... in position ... .

.12   Small fishing boats in area around ... - navigate with caution.

.13   Submarines operating in sea area around ... surface vessels are in attendance.

.1.4   **Route information**

.1   Route ... / Traffic   Lane   ... has been suspended / discontinued / diverted.

.1.5   **Hydrographic information**

.1   Tidal prediction for ... (name of station(s)) / area ... :

   .1.1   A tide of ... metres above / below datum is expected in position ... / area ... at about ... UTC.

   .1.2   Abnormally high / low tides are expected in position ... / area ... at about ... UTC.

.2   The tide is rising -

        ~ it is ... hours before high water / after low water.

        ~ it is ... metres below high water / above low water.

.3   The tide is falling -

        ~ it is ... hours after high water / before low water.

        ~ it is ... metres below high water / above low water.

.4   The tide is slack.

.5   Present tide is ... metres above / below datum ... in position ... ..

.6   The tide is ... metres above / below prediction

.7   The tidal stream / current is ... knots in position ... .

.8   The tide is setting in direction ... degrees.

.9   The depth of water is / is not sufficient in position ... .

.12   Charted depth has increased / decreased by ... metres due to winds / sea state.

.1.6   Electronic navigational aids information

.1   GPS Satellite ... (number) unusable from ... (date and time) to ... (date and time). Cancel one hour after time of restoration.

.2   LORAN station ... (name number of master / slave)

.3   RACON ... (name of station) in position ... off air ... from ... (date and time) to ... (date and time).

.1.7   Meteorological warnings

.1   Gale warning / storm warning was issued at ... UTC starting at ... UTC .

   .1.1   Gale warning / storm warning. Wind at ... UTC in area ... (met. area) from direction... (cardinal points) and force Beaufort ... backing / veering to ... (cardinal points).

.2   Tropical storm warning was issued at ... UTC starting at ... UTC.

   .2.1   Tropical storm warning at ... UTC. Hurricane ... (name) / tropical cyclone / tornado / willy-willy / typhoon / ... with central pressure of ... millibars/hPascals located in position ... .Present movement ... (cardinal points) at ... knots. Winds of ... knots within radius of ... nautical miles of centre. Seas over ... metres. Further information on VHF Channel ... / frequency ... (at ... UTC).

.1.8   Meteorological information

.1 Position of tropical storm ... (name) ..., path   ... (cardinal points), speed of advance ... knots.

.2 Wind direction ... (cardinal points), force Beaufort ... in position ... .

.3 Wind is backing / veering and increasing / decreasing.

.4 Wind is expected to increase / decrease in position ... to force Beaufort ... within the next ... hours.

.5 Visibility in position ...

   ~ ... metres / nautical miles.

~ reduced by mist / fog / snow / dust / rain / ... .

~ expected to increase / decrease to ... metres / nautical miles within the next ... hours.

.6 Sea / swell in position ...

~ ... metres from ... (cardinal points).

~ expected to increase / decrease within the next ... hours.

.7 Icing is expected / not expected in area ... .

.1.9 **Meteorological questions and answers**

See AI/3.1 "Meteorological and hydrological conditions"

.2 **Navigational assistance service**

Shore based pilotage by Navigational Assistance Service: also see AI/6.4 .3.18 to .3.21

.2.1 **Request and identification**

.1 Is shore based radar assistance available?

.1.1 Yes, shore based radar assistance is available.

.1.2 No, shore based radar assistance is not available.

.2 Shore based radar assistance is available from ... to ... UTC.

.3 Do you require navigational assistance to reach ... ?

.3.1 Yes, I require navigational assistance.

.3.2 No, I do not require navigational assistance

.4 What is your position?

.4.1 My position is bearing ... degrees ..., distance ... kilometres / nautical miles from ... .

.5 How was your position obtained?

.5.1 My position was obtained by GPS / RADAR / cross-bearing /

astronomical observation / ...

.6 Repeat your position for identification.

.7 I have located you on my radar screen.

.7.1 Your position is bearing ... degrees, distance ... kilometres / nautical miles from ... .

.8 I cannot locate you on my radar screen.

.9 What is your present course and speed?

.9.1   My present course is ... degrees, my speed is ... knots.

.10   What is the course to reach you?

   .10.1   The course to reach me is ... degrees.

.11   Is your radar in operation?

   .11.1   Yes, my radar is in operation.

   .11.2   No, my radar is not in operation.

.12   What range scale are you using?

   .12.1   I am using ... miles range scale.

   .12.2   Change to a larger / smaller range scale.

.13   You are leaving my radar screen.

.14   Change to radar ... (name) VHF Channel ... .

.15   I have lost radar contact.

.2.2   Position

.1   You are entering ... .

.2   Your position is .../ bearing ... degrees, distance ... kilometres / nautical miles from ... .

.4   You are passing ... .

   You are

      ~ in the centre of the fairway.

      ~ on / not on the radar reference line (of the fairway).

      ~ on the ... (cardinal points) side of the fairway.

.5   You are approaching the ... (cardinal points) limit of the fairway.

.6   Your position is buoy number ... distance ... metres / cables to the ... (cardinal points) of the radar reference line

.7   Your position is distance ... metres / cables from the intersection of radar reference line ... and radar reference line ... and distance ... metres / cables to the ... (cardinal points) of radar reference line ... .

.8   MV ... has reported at reporting point ... .

.9   You are getting closer to the vessel ... (cardinal points) of you.

.10   Vessel on opposite course is passing to the ... (cardinal points) of you.

.11   MV ... is metres / cables ... (cardinal points) of you

      ~ is ingoing / outgoing.

~ has stopped.

~ is at anchor.

~ is on a reciprocal course

~ will overtake to the ... (cardinal points) of you

.12 Vessel has anchored ... metres / cables ... (cardinal points) of you in position ... .

.13 Vessel ... (cardinal points) of you is obstructing your movements.

.14 You will meet crossing traffic in position ... .

.15 Vessel is entering / leaving the fairway at ... .

.16 Buoy ... distance ... metres / cables ... (cardinal points).

.17 Vessel ... (cardinal points) of you is

~ turning.

~ anchoring.

~ increasing / decreasing speed.

~ overtaking you.

~ not under command.

.2.3 **Course**

Note: The user of this phrase should be fully aware of the implications of words such as "track", "heading" and "course made good."

.1 Your track is

~ parallel with the reference line.

~ diverging from the reference line.

~ converging to the reference line.

.2 What is your present course / heading?

.2.1 My present course / heading is ... degrees

.3 You are steering a dangerous course.

.4 Course to make good is ... degrees.

.5 Vessel ... (cardinal points) of you is on same course ... degrees.

.5.1 Advise you

~ Keep your present course.

~ a new course of ... degrees.

.6 Have you altered course?

.6.1   Yes, I have altered course - my new course is... degrees.

.6.2   No, I have not altered course - my course is ... degrees.

.7   You are running into danger -

~ shallow water ... (cardinal points) of you.

~ submerged wreck ... (cardinal points) of you.

~ fog bank ... (cardinal points) of you.

~ risk of collision (with a vessel bearing ... degrees, distance ... kilometres / nautical miles).

~ bridge is defective / ... .

.3   Traffic organization service

.3.1   Clearance, forward planning

.1   Traffic clearance is required before entering ... .

.2   Do not enter the traffic lane / ... .

.3   Proceed to the emergency anchorage.

.4   Keep clear of .../ avoid ... .

.5   You have permission

~ to enter the traffic lane / route - traffic clearance granted.

~ to enter traffic lane / route in position ... at ... UTC.

.6   Do not pass the reporting point ... until ... UTC.

.7   Report at the next way point / way point ... / at ... UTC.

.8   You must arrive at way point ... at ... UTC - your berth is clear.

.9   Do not arrive in position ... before / after ... UTC.

.10   The tide is with you / against you.

.3.2   Anchoring

.1   You must anchor

~ at ... UTC.

~ until the pilot arrives.

~ in a different position.

       ~ clear of fairway.

.2   Do not anchor in position ... .

.3   Anchoring is prohibited.

.6   You must heave up anchor.

.7   You are at anchor in a wrong position.

.8   Have your crew on stand by for heaving up anchor when the pilot embarks.

.9   You have permission to anchor (at ... UTC)

       ~ in position ... .

       ~ until the pilot arrives.

       ~ until the tugs arrive.

       ~ until sufficient water.

.10   You are obstructing the fairway / other traffic.

.11   Are you dragging / dredging anchor?

    .11.1 Yes, I am dragging / dredging anchor.

    .11.2 No, I am not dragging / dredging anchor.

.12   Do not dredge anchor.

.3.3 **Arrival, berthing and departure**

.1   Your orders are to berth on ... .

.2   Your orders are changed to proceed to ... .

.3   Proceed to ... for orders.

.4   You have permission to enter / to proceed at ... UTC.

.5   Vessel is turning / manoeuvering in position ... .

.6   MV ...

       ~ will turn in position ... .

       ~ will leave ... at ... UTC.

       ~ is leaving ... .

       ~ has left ... .

       ~ entered fairway in position ... .

.7   Your berth is not clear (until ... UTC)

    .7.1   Your berth will be clear at ... UTC.

.8   You will berth / dock at ... UTC .

.9   Berthing has been delayed by ... hours.

.10   Be ready to get underway.

    .10.1   I am ready to get underway

.11   Get underway.

.12   Are you underway?

    .12.1   Yes, I am underway.

    .12.2   No, I am not underway.

.13   Move ahead / astern ... metres.

.14   Your vessel is in position - make fast.

.3.4 Enforcement

.1   According to my radar, your course does not comply with Rule 10 of COLREGS.

.2   Your actions will be reported to the Authorities.

.3   You are

     ~ not complying with traffic regulations.

     ~ not keeping to the correct traffic lane.

.4   Have all navigational instruments in operation before entering this area / area ... .

.5   Your navigation lights are not visible.

.6   Recover your fishing gear.

    .6.1   You are fishing in the fairway.

.7   Fishing gear is to the ... (cardinal points) of you.

.8   Fishing in area ...is prohibited.

.9   You are approaching a prohibited fishing area.

.10   Fairway speed is... knots.

.3.5 Avoiding dangerous situations, providing safe movements

.1   It is dangerous

     ~ to anchor in your present position.

     ~ to remain in your present position.

     ~ to alter course to ... (cardinal points).

.2   Large vessel is leaving the fairway- keep clear of the fairway approach.

.3   Nets with buoys / without buoys in this area - navigate with caution.

.4   Collision in position ... .

.5   MV ... is aground / on fire / ... in position ... .

.6   Stand by for assistance.

.7   Vessels must

      ~ keep clear of this area / area ... .

      ~ avoid this area / area ... .

      ~ navigate with caution.

.8   Keep clear of ... - search and rescue in progress.

.9   Your present course is too close

      ~ to ingoing / outgoing vessel.

      ~ to the vessel that you are overtaking.

      ~ to the ... (cardinal points) limit of the fairway.

.10   Your course is deviating from the radar reference line.

.11   You are running into danger

      ~ shallow water .... (cardinal points) of you.

      ~ submerged wreck ... (cardinal points) of you.

      ~ fog bank ... (cardinal points) of you.

      ~ risk of collision (with vessel bearing ... degrees,
            distance ... kilometres / nautical miles).

      ~ bridge is defective.

.12   You are proceeding at a dangerous speed.

.13   You must

      ~ proceed by the fairway / route ... .

      ~ keep to the ... (cardinal points) of the fairway line /
radar reference line.

      ~ stay clear of the fairway.

.14   You must wait for MV ... to cross ahead of you.

.15   You must wait for MV ... to clear ... before

      ~ entering the fairway.

      ~ getting underway.

      ~ leaving the berth.

.16   Do not

      ~ overtake.

      ~ cross the fairway.

.17   Alter course to ...(cardinal points) of you.

.18   Pass ... (cardinal points) of

      ~ ingoing / outgoing / anchored / disabled vessel.

      ~ of ... mark / ... .

.19   Stop engines.

.20   MV ...

> ~ wishes to overtake ... (cardinal points) of you.

> ~ agrees / does not agree to be overtaken.

> ~ is approaching an obscured area ... - approaching vessels acknowledge.

.3.6   Canal and lock operations

.1   You must

> ~ close up on the vessel ahead of you.

> ~ drop back from the vessel ahead of you.

> ~ wait at ... .

> ~ moor at ... .

> ~ wait for lock clearance at ... until ... UTC.

.2   Convoy ... must wait / moor at ... .

.3   You will

> ~ join convoy ... at ... UTC.

> ~ enter canal / lock at ... UTC.

.4   Transit will begin at ... UTC.

.5   Your place in convoy is number ... .

.6   Transit / convoy speed is ... knots.

.7   Convoys / vessels will pass in area ... .

AI/6.3   Handing over to another VTS

.1   ... VTS this is ... VTS: MV ... position is bearing... degrees, distance ... kilometres / nautical miles from ... . working frequency is VHF Channel ... . Your target. Please confirm.

.2   ... VTS this is ... VTS: MV ... position bearing is ... degrees, distance ... kilometres / nautical miles from ... . I confirm. My target.

.3   .... VTS this is ... VTS: MV ... position is bearing... degrees, distance ... kilometres / nautical miles from ... . I am unable to take over this target.

AI/6.4   **Phrases for communication with emergency services and allied services**

.1   **Emergency services** (SAR, fire fighting, pollution fighting)
See AI/1 "Distress Communication"

.2   **Tug services**
Also see AII/3.6 "Tug assistance"

 .1 How many tugs do you require?

  .1.1 I require ... tug(s).

 .2 You must take

    ~ ... tug(s) according to port regulations.

    ~ ... tug(s) fore and ... tug(s) aft.

 .3 Wait for the tug(s) in position ... .

 .4 The tugs will meet you in position ... at ... UTC.

 .6 Tug services have been suspended until ...(date and time) / resumed on...(date and time).

.3   **Pilot request**

 .1 Must I take a pilot?

  .1.1 Yes, you must take a pilot - pilotage is compulsory.

  .1.2 No, you need not take a pilot.

 .2 Do you require a pilot?

  .2.1 Yes, I require a pilot.

  .2.2 No, I do not require a pilot - I am holder of Pilotage Exemption Certificate (No. ...).

 .3 You are exempted from pilotage.

 .4 Do you require a pilot at ...(name) Pilot Station?

  .4.1 Yes, I require a pilot at ...(name) Pilot Station.

  .4.2 No, I do not require a pilot at ...(name) Pilot Station - I require a pilot in position ...

 .5 What is your ETA at ...(name) Pilot Station in local time?

  .5.1 My ETA at...(name) Pilot Station is ... hours local time.

 .6 What is local time?

  .6.1 Local time is ... hours.

 .7 What is your position?

   .7.1 My position is ... .

 .8   What is your distance from ...(name) Pilot Station?

   .8.1 My distance from ...(name) Pilot Station is ... kilometres / nautical miles.

 .9   Is the pilot boat on station?

   .9.1 Yes, the pilot boat is on station.

   .9.2 No, the pilot boat is not on station.

   .9.3 The pilot boat will be on station at ... hours local time.

 .10 In what position can I take the pilot?

   .10.1 Take the pilot at ...(Pilot Station) / near ... at ... hours local time.

 .11 When will the pilot embark?

   .11.1 The pilot will embark at ... hours local time.

 .12 The pilot boat is coming to you.

 .13 Stop in present position and wait for the pilot.

 .14 Keep the pilot boat ... (cardinal points) of you.

 .15 What is your freeboard?

   .15.1 My freeboard is ... metres.

 .16 Change to VHF Channel ... for pilot transfer.

 .17 Stand by on VHF Channel ... until pilot transfer is completed.

 .18 Pilotage at ...(name) Pilot Station has been suspended until ... (date and local time).

 .19 Pilotage at ...(name) Pilot Station has been resumed.

 .20 The pilot cannot embark at ... (name) Pilot Station due to ... .

 .21 Do you accept shore-based navigational assistance from VTS Centre?

   .21.1 Yes, I accept shore-based navigational assistance.

   .21.2 No, I do not accept shore-based navigational assistance.

   .21.3 I will stay in position ... until ... .

 .22 You have permission to proceed by yourself (or wait for the pilot at ... buoy).

 .23 Follow the pilot boat inward where the pilot will embark.

 .4 **Embarking / disembarking pilot**
   See AI/4.2 "Embarking/disembarking pilot"

AII   ON-BOARD COMMUNICATION PHRASES (A)

AII/1   Standard Wheel Orders

All wheel orders given should be repeated by the helmsman and the officer of the watch should ensure that they are carried out correctly and immediately. All wheel orders should be held until countermanded. The helmsman should report immediately if the vessel does not answer the wheel.

When there is concern that the helmsman is inattentive s/he should be questioned:

"What is your heading ?"   And s/he should respond:
"My heading is ... degrees."

Order	Meaning
1. Midships	Rudder to be held in the fore and aft position.
2. Port / starboard five	5° of port / starboard rudder to be held.
3. Port / starboard ten	10° of port / starboard rudder to be held.
4. Port / starboard fifteen	15° of port / starboard rudder to be held.
5 Port / starboard twenty	20° of port / starboard rudder to be held.
6. Port / starboard twenty-five	25° of port / starboard rudder to be held.
7. Hard -a-port / starboard	Rudder to be held fully over to port / starboard.
8. Nothing to port/starboard	Avoid allowing the vessel's head to go to port/starboard
9. Meet her	Check the swing of the vessel´s head in a turn.
10. Steady	Reduce swing as rapidly as possible.
11. Ease to five / ten / fifteen / twenty	Reduce amount of rudder to 5°/10°/15°/20° and hold.

12. Steady as she goes
Steer a steady course on the compass heading indicated at the time of the order. The helmsman is to repeat the order and call out the compass heading on receiving the order. When the vessel is steady on that heading, the helmsman is to call out: "Steady on ..."

13. Keep the buoy/ mark/ beacon/ ... on port side / starboard side.

14. Report if she does not answer the wheel.

15. Finished with wheel, no more steering.

When the officer of the watch requires a course to be steered by compass, the direction in which s/he wants the wheel turned should be stated followed by each numeral being said separately, including zero, for example:

Order Course to be steered

Port, steer one eight two	182°
Starboard, steer zero eight two	082°
steer three zero five	305°

On receipt of an order to steer, for example, 1820, the helmsman should repeat it and bring the vessel round steadily to the course ordered. When the vessel is steady on the course ordered, the helmsman is to call out:
"Steady on one eight two".
The person giving the order should acknowledge the helmsman's reply.

If it is desired to steer on a selected mark the helmsman should be ordered to:
"Steer on ... buoy / ... mark / ... beacon".
The person giving the order should acknowledge the helmsman's reply.

AII/2 Standard Engine Orders

Any engine order given should be repeated by the person operating the bridge telegraph(s) and the officer of the watch should ensure the order is carried out correctly and immediately.

Order

1. (Port / starboard engines) Full ahead / astern
2. (Port / starboard engines) Half ahead / astern
3. (Port / starboard engines) Slow ahead / astern
4. (Port / starboard engines) Dead slow ahead / astern
5. Stop (port / starboard) engines
6. Emergency full ahead / astern
7. Stand by engine
   (Engine-room personnel fully ready to manoeuver and bridge manned to relay engine orders.)
8. Finished with engines – no more manoeuvering.
   (Operation of engines no longer required.)

In vessels fitted with twin propellers, the word "both" should be added to all orders affecting both shafts, e.g. "Full ahead both", and "Slow astern both", except that the words "Stop all engines" should be used, when appropriate. When required to manoeuver twin propellers independently, this should be indicated, i.e. "Full ahead starboard", "Half astern port", etc.

Where bow thrusters are used, the following orders are used:

9. Bow thruster full / half to port / starboard.
10. Stern thruster full / half to port / starboard.
11. Bow / stern thruster stop

AII/3 Pilot on the Bridge

AII/3.1 Propulsion system

.1   Is the engine a diesel or a turbine?

   .1.1   The engine is a diesel / turbine.

.2   Is the engine-room manned or is the engine on bridge control?

   .2.1   The engine-room is manned.

.2.2   The engine is on bridge control.

.3   How long does it take to change the engines from ahead to astern?

    .3.1   It takes ... seconds to change the engines (from ahead to astern).

.4   How long does it take to start the engines from stopped?

    .4.1   It takes ... seconds to start the engines (from stopped).

.5   Is extra power available in an emergency?

    .5.1   Yes, extra power is available.

    .5.2   No, extra power is not available.

.6   Do you have a controllable or fixed pitch propeller?

    .6.1   We have a controllable pitch propeller.

    .6.2   We have a fixed pitch propeller.

.7   Do you have a right-hand or left - hand propeller?

    .7.1   We have a right-hand / left-hand propeller.

.8   Do you have a single propeller or twin propellers?

    .8.1   We have a single propeller / twin propellers.

.9   Do you have a bow thrusteror stern thruster?

    .9.1   We have one /two/.. bow thruster(s) / stern thruster(s).

.10   What is the maximum manoeuvering power ahead / astern?

    .10.1   The maximum manoeuvering power ahead / astern is ... kilo Watts.

.11   What are the maximum revolutions ahead / astern?

    .11.1   The maximum revolutions ahead / astern are ... .

.12   Do the twin propellers turn inward or outward when going ahead.

    .12.1   The twin propellers turn inward / outward (when going ahead).

AII/3.2 manoeuvering

.1   I require the pilot card / manoeuvering data.

.2   What is the diameter of the turning circle?

    .2.1   The diameter of the turning circle is ... metres.

.3   What is the advance and transfer distance in a crash-stop?

    .3.1   The advance distance is ... kilometres / nautical miles, the transfer distance is ... degrees (in a crash-stop).

.4   How long does it take from hard-a-port to hard-a-starboard?

.4.1   It   takes   ...   seconds   (from   hard-a-port   to hard-a-starboard).

.5   Is the turning effect of the propeller very strong?

　　.5.1   Yes, the turning effect (of the propeller) is very strong.

　　.5.2   No, the turning effect (of the propeller) is   not very strong.

.6   Where is the whistle control?

　　.6.1   The whistle control is on the console / on ... .

.7   What notice is required to reduce from full sea speed to manoeuvering speed?

　　.7.1   ... minutes notice is required (to reduce from full sea speed to manoeuvering speed).

.8   Do you have an automatic pilot?

　　.8.1   Yes, we have an automatic pilot.

　　.8.2   No, we do not have an automatic pilot.

.9   Give ... short / prolonged blast(s) (on the whistle).

.10   Stand by lookout.

.11   Maintain a speed of ... knots.

.12   What is the (manoeuvering) speed at full / half / slow / dead slow ahead?

　　.12.1   The manoeuvering speed at full / half / slow / dead slow ahead is ... knots.

.13   What is the full sea speed / fairway speed?

　　.13.1   The full sea speed / fairway speed is ... knots.

AII/3.3 Radar

.1   Is the radar operational?

　　.1.1   Yes, the radar is operational.

　　.1.2   No, the radar is not operational.

.2   Where is the radar antenna?

　　.2.1   The radar antenna is on ... .

.3   Does the radar have any blind sectors?

　　.3.1   Yes, the radar has blind sectors from ... to ... degrees and from ... to ... degrees.

　　.3.2   No, the radar does not have any blind sectors.

.4   Change the radar to

　　~ ... miles range scale.

~ relative head-up / north-up / course-up.

~ true-motion north-up / course-up.

AII/3.4 Draft and air draft

.1   What is your present maximum draft?

　　.1.1   My present maximum draft is … metres.

　　.1.2   My draft forward / aft is … metres.

.2   What is your air draft?

　　.2.1   My air draft is … metres.

AII/3.5 Anchoring

.1   **Going to anchor**

　　.1   Stand by port / starboard / both anchor(s) for letting go.

　　.2   Walk out the anchor(s)

　　.3   We are going to anchorage.

　　.4   We will let go port / starboard / both anchor(s).

　　.5   Put … shackles in the water / in the pipe / on deck.

　　.6   Walk back port / starboard / both anchor(s) one / one and a half shackle(s).

　　.7   We will let go port / starboard / both anchor(s) … shackle(s) and dredge it / them.

　　.8   Let go port / starboard / both anchor(s).

　　.9   Slack out the cable(s).

　　.9.1   Check the cable(s).

　　.9.2   Hold on the port / the starboard / both cable(s).

　.10   How is the cable leading?

　　.10.1   The cable is leading

　　　　~ ahead / astern.

　　　　~ to port / to starboard.

　　　　~ round the bow.

　　　　~ up and down.

　.11   How is the cable growing?

　　.11.1   The cable is slack / tight / coming tight.

　.12   Is / are the anchor(s) holding.

　　.12.1   Yes, the anchor(s) is / are holding.

.12.2   No, the anchor(s) is / are not holding.

.13   Is she brought up?

.13.1   Yes, she is brought up in position … .

.13.2   No, she is not brought up (yet).

.14   Switch on the anchor light(s).

.15   Hoist the anchor ball.

.16   Check the anchor position by bearings / by … .

.16.1   The anchor position is bearing … degrees, distance …
kilometres / nautical miles to … .

.16.2   Check the anchor position every … minutes.

.2   **Leaving the anchorage**

.1   How much cable is out?

.1.1   … shackle(s) is / are   out.

.2   Stand by for heaving up.

.3   Put the windlass in gear.

.3.1   The windlass is in gear.

.4   How is the cable leading?

.4.1   The cable is leading

~ ahead / astern.

~ to port / to starboard.

~ round the bow.

~ up and down.

.5   Heave up port / starboard / both cable(s).

.6   How much weight is on the cable?

.6.1   Much / too much weight is on the cable.

.6.2   No weight is on the cable.

.7   Stop heaving.

.8   How many shackles are left (to come in)?

.8.1   ... shackles are left (to come in).

.9   Attention! Turn in cable(s).

.10   The anchor(s) is / are aweigh..

.10.1   The cables are clear.

.11   The anchor(s) is / are clear of the water / home / foul /
secured.

AII/3.6 Tug assistance

.1 We will take ... tug(s).

.2 The tug(s) will pull / push.

.3 We use the towing line(s) of your vessel.

  .3.1 We use the towing line(s) of the tug(s).

.4 Stand by for making fast the tug(s).

.5 Use the centre lead / panama lead.

  .5.1 Use the fairlead

    ~ on port side / starboard side.

    ~ amidships.

    ~ on port bow / starboard bow.

    ~ on port / starboard quarter.

.6 Send heaving line(s) to the tug(s).

.7 Send two towing line(s) to the tug(s).

.8 Lower towing line(s)

    ~ to the tug(s).

    ~ ... metre(s) from the water.

.9 Slack away towing line(s).

.10 Make fast the tug(s).

  .10.1 Make fast the tug(s)

    ~ forward / aft.

    ~ on port bow / starboard bow.

    ~ on port quarter / starboard quarter.

.11 Make fast the forward / aft tug(s) alongside on port side / starboard side.

.12 Make fast ... tug(s) on each bow / quarter.

.13 Put the eyes of the towing line(s) on bitts.

.14 The tug(s) is / are fast (on ...).

.15 Keep clear of towing line(s).

.16 Stand by for letting go the tug(s).

.17 Let go the tug(s).

.18 Towing line(s) is/are broken.

AII/3.7 Berthing and unberthing

.1   **General**

    .1   Is/are the propeller(s) clear?

        .1.1   Yes, the propeller(s) is clear.

        .1.2   No, the propeller(s) is not clear.

        .1.3   Keep the propeller(s) clear.

    .2   Are fenders on the berth?

        .2.1   Yes, fenders are on the berth.

        .2.2   No, fenders are not on the berth.

    .3   Have fenders ready fore and aft.

.2   **Berthing**

    .1   We will berth port side / starboard side alongside.

    .2   We will moor

        ~ to buoy(s) (ahead and astern).

        ~ alongside.

        ~ to dolphins.

    .3   Send out

        ~ the head / stern / breast lines.

        ~ the ... spring(s) forward / aft.

    .4   Do you have tension winches?

        .4.1   Yes, we have tension winches (forward and aft).

        4.2   No, we do not have tension winches.

    .5   Have the heaving lines ready forward and aft.

    .6   Send the heaving / head / stern / breast line(s) ashore.

    .7   The linesmen will use shackles / lashings for securing the mooring.

    .8   Use

        ~ the centre lead / panama lead .

        ~ the bow lead.

        ~ the port quarter / starboard quarter lead.

    .9   Heave on the ... line(s) / ... spring(s)..

    .10   Pick up the slack on the ... line(s) / ... spring(s)..

    .11   Heave away.

.11.1   Stop heaving.

.12   Slack away / Check the ... line(s) / ... spring(s)..

.13   Hold on the ... line(s) / ... spring(s).

.14   Heave in easy.

  .14.1   Heave alongside.

.15   Keep the ... line(s) / ... spring(s) tight.

.16   Report the forward / aft distance to ... .

  .16.1   The forward / aft distance to ... ... is metres.

.17   We have to move ... metres ahead / astern.

.18   We are in position.

.19   Make fast fore and aft.

.20   Finished with manoeuvering stations.

.3   **Unberthing**

.1   Stand by engine(s).

.2   Are you ready to get underway?

  .2.1   Yes, we are ready (to get underway).

  .2.2   No, we are not ready (yet) (to get underway).

  .2.3   We will be ready to get underway in ... minutes.

.3   Stand by for letting go.

.4   Single up the ... lines and ... springs fore and aft.

.5   Slack away / hold on / heave on the

    ~ head / stern line.

    ~ breast line.

    ~ fore / aft spring.

.6   Let go

    ~ the head / stern line.

    ~ the breast line.

    ~ the fore / aft spring

    ~ all (forward / aft).

.7   Let go the towing line(s).

.8   Stand by bow anchor(s).

.9   Finished with manoeuvering stations.

Annex(2)   MV Hyundai Jakarta 호 항해일지

	TO/AT	KAOHSIUNG	ZD	−09.0	PAGE	3

Remarks

0400　ROUND MADE ALL IN ALL.& DECK AREA. CHECKED GANGWAY & MOORING LINE CONDITION.
　　　ALL'S WELL　　　　　　　　　　　　　　　　　　　　　　　　　2/0

0800　ROUND MADE ALL IN ALL.& DECK AREA. CHECKED GANGWAY & MOORING LINE CONDITION. ALL'S WELL.
　　　　　　　　　　　　　　　　　　　　　　　　　　　　2/0(0)

1200　ROUND MADE IN ALL ACC.& DECK AREA. CHECKED GANGWAY. & MOORING LINE CONDITION. ALL'S WELL.
　　　　　　　　　　　　　　　　　　　　　　　　　　　2/0(0)

1230　MASTER ON THE BRIDGE

(1230 − 1300)　PRIOR TO DEP. 'QOE', CHECKED & TESTED NO.1 & NO.2 AUTO PILOT SYS. CONTROL SYS. OF ALL THE REMOTE
　　　　S/G SYS. EM'CY POWER SUPPLY & CONTROL SYS. POWER FAILURE ALARM WHILE OBSERVING S/G AND
　　　　THE EQUIP. LINKED. POWER UNIT FAILURE ALARM. COMM. EQUIP BETWEEN THE BRIDGE & S/G RM, RUDDER
　　　　ANGLE INDICATOR. DIFF, BETWEEN S/G RM & THE BRIDGE. GMDSS SYS. WHISTLES. NAVI DECK LIGHTS,
　　　　SHIP'S COMM. SYS. ALARM SYS. STORAGE BATTS AND ALL NAV. EQUIP. AS PER COMPANY'S CHECK LIST
　　　　N1, N4 & 33 CFR 164.25 & SOLAS CH.5 REG 26. FOUND IN GOOD.

(1257)　COM'TED CARGO OPERATION.

(1300)　S.B.E　　　　　　　　　　1300−1370 CONDUCTED MPP BRIEFING BEFORE DEP. QOE.

(1310)　TESTED M/E PROPULSION AHD/AST. THE FULL RUDDER ANGLE MOVEMENT AND TIME TAKEN FOR THE
　　　RUDDER. ALL'S WELL.

1315　P.O.B (2P)　　　　　　　　1317　ALL S/BY

1324　TOOK TUG ON PORT Q'TER & BOW

(1330)　ALL LINE LET GO

1358　TUGS AWAY

1535　P.L.H (2P)

1550　CHECKED FRRF CNTR'S TEMP.& CONDITION. ALL'S WELL

(1600)　R/UP ENG. AT 10-14.0N, 107-10.9E

FO/AT	KAOHSIUNG	ZD	-07.0	PAGE	4

Remarks

0005 TESTED AUTO PILOT SYS TO HAND & N.F.U. MODE. FOUND IN GOOD.
0010 ROUND MADE ON ACC. AREA FOR FIRE & SAFETY. TTL 23 CREWS ONBOARD. ALL'S WELL.

0400 KEPT A SHARP LOOKOUT THROUGH THE WATCH.   2/O
0410 TESTED AUTO PILOT SYS. TO HAND & NFU MODE. FOUND IN GOOD
0420 ROUND MADE ALL IN ALL & E/R AREA FOR FIRE. SAFETY & SECURITY. TTL 23 CREWS ONBOARD.
ALL'S WELL.

0800 KEPT A SHARP LOOKOUT THROUGH THE WATCH.   C/O
0805 TESTED AUTO PILOT SYS. TO HAND & NFU MODE. FOUND IN GOOD.
0830 CHECKED RF CNTR'S TEMP. & CONDITION.

1200 KEPT A SHARP LOOK OUT THROUGH THE WATCH   3/O(A)
1205 TESTED AUTO PILOT SYS. TO HAND & NFU MODE. FOUND IN GOOD.

1300-1330 (1400) CARRIED OUT SANITARY INSP. IN BRIDGE, ALL & E/R AREA INCLUDE FOOD & CATERING BY
MASTER & HEAD OF DEPARTMENT ACCORDING TO THE RELEVANT CHECK LIST. TESTED &
CHECKED AIR ELEC. WHISTLES, F.D.S, GA, COMM. SYS, HOSPITAL ALARM, RF CHAMBER ALARM
GENERAL CONDITION SATISFACTORY AND CARRIED OUT ROUTINE VISUAL INSP. FOR VGP IN
ALLORDANCE WITH CHECK LIST. DEFFICIENLY NOTED & DULEY AMENDED.
1400-1500 (1330-1400) WEEKLY CARRIED OUT MONTHLY INSP. TESTED EM'LY FIRE P/P, GENERAL EM'LY ALARM, COMM. C/O
SYS & P.A & VISUAL INSP. FOR L/BOAT & L/RAFT AND MOVING TEST OF L/BOAT LAUNCHING
DEVILES FROM STOWED PSN AND TESTED OPERATION OF L/BOAT ENG. AHD/AST. FOR 3 MINS.
ALL'S WELL.

1550 CHECKED RF CNTR'S TEMP & CONDITION.
1600 KEPT A SHARP LOOK OUT THROUGH THE WATCH   2/O
1605 TESTED AUTOPILOT SYS. TO HAND & NFU MODE. FOUND IN GOOD.

2000 KEPT A SHARP LOOKOUT THRU THE WATCH.   3/O(B)
2005 TESTED AUTO PILOT SYS. TO HAND & NFU MODE. FOUND IN GOOD.
2100 1 HR ADVANCED ALL SHIP'S CLOCK TO MEET ZD: -08.0

2400 KEPT A SHARP LOOK OUT THRU THE WATCH.   3/O(A)

08TH APR. 2019 ⟨MON⟩

⟨1000-1100⟩ HELD ON NO.2 LIFE BOAT (RESCUE BOAT) LAUNCHING DRILL ON THE WATER LEVEL AT 'KHH'.
SOUNDED SIGNAL FOR ABANDON SHIP DRILL. ALL CREW MUSTERED AT EACH BOAT DECK. CHECKED CREW'S
EFFECTS, DRESSING & DONNING L/JACKET. PREPARED TO LOWER NO.2 LIFE BOAT. AND TESTED ALL
EQUIPMENT OF LIFE BOAT AND DAVIT AND EM'CY LIGHT FOR LAUNCHING STN THEN CREW EMBARKED.
LOWERED NO.2 LIFE BOAT ON THE WATER AND RELEASED BOAT HOOKS & MANOEUVERED IN THE WATER
AND TESTED ENG. WITH FULL SPEED. RAISED & SECURED NO.2 LIFE BOAT BY CAPT'S ORDER. C/O
INSTRUCTED CREW ABOUT HOW TO LOWER & HOIST LIFE BOAT, RESCUE BOAT & LIFE RAFT AND HOW TO
OPERATE BOAT ENG. ALL CREW UNDERSTOOD WELL.

⟨1312⟩ TURNED OFF AIS DUE TO BLACKOUT TEST.
⟨1356⟩ TURNED ON AIS AFTER FINISHED BLACKOUT TEST.
1500-1510 CONDUCTED MPP BRIEFING BEFORE DEP. 'KHH' ALL'S WELL.
1600 CHECKED RF CNTR'S TEMP. & CONDITION.
1600 ROUND MADE ALL IN ACC & DECK AREA. CHECKED GANGWAY & MOORING LINE CONDITION. ALL'S WELL. 2/O ⟨sig⟩
1605 MASTER ON THE BRIDGE.
⟨1630-1700⟩ PRIOR TO DEP. 'KHH', CHECKED & TESTED NO.1 & NO.2 AUTO PILOT SYS, CONTROL SYS, OP. ALL THE REMOTE
SIG SYS. EM'CY PWR SUPPLY & CONTROL SYS. PWR FAILURE ALARM WHILE OBSERVING S/G AND THE EQUIP.
LINKED, PWR UNIT FAILURE ALARM, COMM. EQUIP. BETWEEN THE BRIDGE & S/G RM, RUDDER ANGLE
INDI. DIFF. BETWEEN S/G RM & THE BRIDGE. GMDSS SYS, WHISTLES, NAV./DECK LIGHTS, SHIP'S COMM. SYS,
ALARM SYS, STORAGE BATS AND ALL NAV. EQUIP. AS PER COMPANY'S CHECK LIST N1, N4 & CFR 164.25,
SOLAS CH5. REG 26. FOUND IN GOOD.
⟨1706⟩ ALL S/BY ENG.
1712 COM'TED CARGO OPERATION.
1716 TESTED M/E PROPULSION AHD/AST. THE FULL RUDDER ANGLE MOVEMENT AND TIME TAKEN FOR THE RUDDER
ALL'S WELL
1727 P.O.B ⟨1P⟩
1733 TOOK TUG ON PORT Q'TR
⟨1754⟩ ALL LINE LET GO.   1806 TUG AWAY
1818 P.L.H ⟨1P⟩
⟨1836⟩ R/UP ENG. AT 22-33.0N, 120-12.9E
⟨1842⟩ PASSED ECA (OUT BOUND) AT 22-33.2N, 120-12.6E
⟨1848⟩ STARTED & COM'TED BUNKER CHANGE FROM LSFO TO HSFO AT 22-34.0N, 120-11.2E
1940 MASTER LEFT THE BRIDGE & HAND OVER THE WATCH TO OOW.
2000 KEPT A SHARP LOOK OUT THROUGH THE WATCH.   3/O(B) ⟨sig⟩
2005 TESTED AUTO PILOT SYS. TO HAND & NFU MODE. FOUND IN GOOD.

2400 KEPT A SHARP LOOK OUT THROUGH THE WATCH.   3/O(A) ⟨sig⟩

_____   _____
     Ch. Officer   Master

TO/AT	PUSAN		ZD	-08.0		PAGE	7

Remarks

0005	TESTED AUTO PILOT SYS TO HAND & N.F.U. MODE. FOUND IN GOOD.
0010	ROUND MADE ON ACC. AREA FOR FIRE & SAFETY. TTL 23 CREWS ONBOARD. ALL'S WELL.
0400	KEPT A SHARP LOOKOUT THROUGH THE WATCH. 2/0
0405	TESTED AUTO PILOT SYS. TO HAND & NFU MODE. FOUND IN GOOD
0415	ROUND MADE IN ACC. ALL & E/R AREA FOR SAFETY, FIRE, SECURITY. TTL 23 CREWS ON BOARD. ALL'S WELL
0800	KEPT A SHARP LOOK OUT THROUGH THE WATCH
0805	TESTED AUTO PILOT SYS. TO HAND & NFU MODE. FOUND IN GOOD.
0830	CHECKED RF CNTR'S TEMP. & CONDITION.
1200	KEPT A SHARP LOOK OUT THROUGH THE WATCH 3/0(A)
1205	TESTED AUTO PILOT SYS TO HAND & N.F.U. MODE. FOUND IN GOOD.
1550	CHECKED CONDITION OF RF CNTRS.
1600	KEPT A SHARP LOOKOUT THROUGH THE WATCH. 2/0
1605	TESTED AUTO PILOT SYS. TO HAND & NFU MODE. FOUND IN GOOD.
2000	KEPT A SHARP LOOKOUT THRU THE WATCH. 3/0(B)
2005	TESTED AUTO PILOT SYS. TO HAND & NFU MODE. FOUND IN GOOD.
2100	ADVANCED ALL SHIP'S CLOCK 1 HR TO MEET ZD: -09.0
2400	KEPT A SHARP LOOK OUT THROUGH THE WATCH. 3/0(A)

Ch. Officer		Master	

| TO (AT) | PUSAN | ZD | -09.0 | PAGE | 9 |

Remarks

0005 TESTED AUTO PILOT SYS TO HAND & N.F.U. MODE, FOUND IN GOOD.

0010 ROUND MADE ON ACC. AREA FOR FIRE & SAFETY. TTL 23 CREWS ONBOARD. ALL'S WELL.

0400 KEPT A SHARP LOOKOUT THROUGH THE WATCH.   2/0

0405 TESTED AUTO PILOT SYS. TO HAND & NFU 170DP. FOUND IN GOOD.

0415 ROUND MADE IN ACC & E/R AREA FOR FIRE, SECURITY, SAFETY. TTL 23 CREWS ONBOARD. ALL'S WELL.

0800 KEPT A SHARP LOOK OUT THROUGH THE WATCH.

0805 TESTED AUTO PILOT SYS. TO HAND & NFU MODE. FOUND IN GOOD

0820 CHECKED RF CNTR'S TEMP. & CONDITION. ALL'S WELL.

〈0820-0850〉 PRIOR TO ARR 'PUS'. CHECKED & TESTED NO.1 & NO.2 AUTO PILOT SYS, CONTROL SYS. OF ALL THE REMOTE S/G
          SYS. EM'CY POWER SUPPLY & CONTROL SYS, POWER FAILURE ALARM WHILE OBSERVING S/G AND THE EQUIP.
          LINKED POWER UNIT FAILURE ALARM. COMM. EQUIP BETWEEN THE BRIDGE & S/G RM. RUDDER ANGLE INDI.
          DIFF. BETWEEN S/G RM & THE BRIDGE. GMDSS SYS. WHISTLES, NAV/DECK LIGHTS, SHIP'S COMM SYS, ALARM
          SYS. STORAGE BATS AND ALL NAV. EQUIP. AS PER COMPANY'S CHECK LIST N1. N4 & 33 CFR 164.25 &
          SOLAS CH.5, REG 26. FOUND IN GOOD.

0900 MASTER ON THE BRIDGE   0905 MASTER STARTED COMMAND THE VSL.

〈1036〉 S.B.E AT 34-45.1N, 128-52.5E 〈DTG: 13'〉

〈1040〉 TESTED M/E PROPULSION AHD/AST. THE FULL RUDDER ANGLE MOVEMENT AND TIME TAKEN FOR THE RUDDER.
       ALL'S WELL.

1206 P.O.B 〈IP〉   1219 ALL S/BY

1240 TOOK TUG ON PORT Q'TR

〈1312〉 FIRST LINE TO PIER   〈1318〉 ALL LINE MADE FAST.

〈1324〉 F.W.E   1326 TUG AWAY & P.L.H 〈IP〉

1328 MASTER LEFT THE BRIDGE

〈1330〉 FSC INSPECTOR 〈IP〉 & P&I SURVEYER ONBOARD.

〈1345〉 BUNKER BARGE ALONGSIDE

1346 COM'CED CARGO OPERATION.

1400 NEWLY JOINED CREW ON-BOARD 〈C/O: PARK J.H〉

| Ch. Officer | | Master | |

	TO/AT	LONG BEACH	ZD	-09.0	PAGE	10

Remarks

0200 SIGN-OFF CREW C/O <PAK S.H> DISEMBARKED

0400 ROUND MADE IN ALL ACC. & DECK AREA. CHECKED GANGWAY & MOORING LINE CONDITION. ALL'S WELL. 2/0

0500 MASTER ON THE BRIDGE

0500-0510 CONDUCTED MPP BRIEFING BEFORE DEP. PUS. ALL'S WELL.

<0500-0530> PRIOR TO DEP. PUS. CHECKED & TESTED AUTO PILOT NO.1 & NO.2 SYS. CONTROL SYS. OF ALL THE REMOTE STG SYS. EM'CY POWER SUPPLY & CONTROL SYS. POWER FAILURE ALARM WHILE OBSERVING STG AND THE EQUIP. LINKED. POWER UNIT FAILURE ALARM, COMM. EQUIP. BETWEEN THE BRIDGE & E/G RM. RUDDER ANGLE INDICATOR DIFF. BETWEEN STG RM & THE BRIDGE., GMDSS SYS. WHISTLES, NAV/DECK LIGHTS, SHIP'S COMM. SYS. ALARM SYS. STORAGE BATTS AND ALL NAV. EQUIP. AS PER COMPANY'S CHECK LIST N1. N4 13YR 16425 & SOLAS CH.5 REG.26. FOUND IN GOOD.

<0536> S.B.E <DTG: 5318'>

0540 P.O.B <IP>

<0546> TESTED M/E PROPULSION AHD/AST. THE FULL RUDDER ANGLE MOVEMENT AND TIME FOR TAKEN THE RUDDER ALL'S WELL.

0548 ALL S/BY   0550 COM'TED C&O OPERATION.

0555 TOOK TUG ON PORT Q'TR

<0600> ALL LINE LET GO.

0624 TUG AWAY   0630 P.L.H <IP>

0800 KEPT A SHARP LOOK OUT THROUGH THE WATCH   3/O(A)

<0824> R/UP ENG AT 34-57.2N, 129-15.2E <DTG: 5285', H: 30.4'>

0830 CHECKED RF CNTR'S TEMP. & CONDITION. ALL'S WELL

0900

1000 MASTER LEFT THE BRIDGE & HAND OVER THE WATCH TO O.O.W

1200 KEPT A SHARP LOOK OUT THROUGH THE WATCH.   3/O(A)

1205 TESTED AUTO PILOT SYS TO HAND & N.F.U. MODE. FOUND IN GOOD

1550 CHECKED RF CNTR'S TEMP. & CONDITION. FOUND IN GOOD.

1600 KEPT A SHARP LOOKOUT THRU THE WATCH.   2/O

1605 TESTED AUTO-PILOT SYS. TO HAND & NFU MODE. FOUND IN GOOD.

2000 KEPT A SHARP LOOKOUT THRU THE WATCH.   3/O(B)

2005 TESTED AUTO PILOT SYS TO HAND & NFU MODE. FOUND IN GOOD.

2100 ADVANCED ALL SHIP'S CLOCK 1HR TO MEET ZD: -10.0

2400 KEPT A SHARP LOOK OUT THROUGH THE WATCH   3/O(A)

Ch. Officer		Master	

| (TO)/AT | LONG BEACH | ZD | -10.0 | PAGE | 11 |

Remarks

0005 TESTED AUTO PILOT SYS TO HAND & N.F.U. MODE. FOUND IN GOOD.

0010 ROUN MADE ON ACC AREA FOR FIRE & SAFETY. TTL 23 CREWS ONBOARD. ALL'S WELL.

0400 KEPT A SHARP LOOKOUT THROUGH THE WATCH.   2/0

0405 TESTED AUTO PILOT SYS TO HAND & NFU MODE, FOUND IN GOOD.

0420 ROUND MADE ALL ACC AREA & E/R FOR SAFETY & SECURITY. ALL'S WELL.

0800 KEPT A SHARP LOOKOUT THROUGH THE WATCH.   C/O

0805 TESTED AUTO PILOT SYS. TO HAND & NFU MODE. ALL'S WELL

0830 CHECKED RF CNTR'S TEMP. & CONDITION. ALL'S WELL.

0900 CHECKED LASHING CONDITION. RETIGHTED LASHING MATERIALS OF ALL BAYS. ALL'S WELL.

1200 KEPT A SHARP LOOK OUT THROUGH THE WATCH.   3/O(A)

1205 TESTED AUTO PILOT SYS TO HAND & N.F.U. MODE. FOUND IN GOOD

(1300-1400) CARRIED OUT SANITARY INSPECTION IN BRIDGE, ACC & E/R AREA INCLUDE FOOD & CATERING BY MASTER & HEAD OF DEPARTMENT ACCORDING TO THE RELEVANT CHECK LIST. TESTED & CHECKED AIR ELEC, WHISTLES, F.D.S, G/A, COMM. SYS., HOSPITAL ALARM, RF CHAMBER ALARM. GENERAL CONDITION SATISFACTORY AND CARRIED OUT ROUTINE VISUAL INSPECTION FOR VGP IN ACCORDANCE WITH CHECK LIST. DEFICIENCIES NOTED & DULY REMEDIED.

(1400-1500) C/O EDUCATED ALL DECK OFFICERS ABOUT BALLAST WATER MANAGEMENT & EXCHANGE. ALL DECK OFFICERS UNDERSTOOD WELL.

(1500-1600) CARRIED OUT WEEKLY INSPECTION. TESTED EM'CY FIRE PUMP, GENERAL ALARM, VISUAL INSPECTION FOR L/RAFT & L/BOAT & THER LAUNCHING DEVICES, MOVING TEST FROM STOWED PSN OF L/BOAT DAVITS, OPERATION OF L/BOAT ENG. AHD/AST FOR 3MIN'S. ALL'S WELL

1550 CHECKED RF CNTR'S TEMP. & CONDITION. ALL'S WELL

1600 KEPT A SHARP LOOK OUT THROUGH THE WATCH.   2/0

1605 TESTED AUTO PILOT SYS TO HAND & NFU MODE. FOUND IN GOOD.

2000 KEPT A SHARP LOOKOUT THRU THE WATCH.   3/O(B)

2005 TESTED AUTO PILOT SYS. TO HAND & NFU MODE. FOUND IN GOOD

2100 ADVANCED ALL SHIP'S CLOCK 1 HR TO MEET ZD: -11.0

2400 KEPT A SHARP LOOK OUT THROUGH THE WATCH.   3/O(A)

| Ch. Officer | | Master | |

| TO/AT | LONG BEACH | ZD | +12.0 | PAGE | 14 |

Remarks

~~0001 READTED 1 DAY SO THAT IS 15TH APR. (MON).~~
0005 TESTED AUTO PILOT SYS TO HAND & N.F.U. MODE. FOUND IN GOOD.
0010 ROUND MADE ON ACC. AREA FOR FIRE & SAFETY. TTL 23 CREWS ONBOARD. ALL'S WELL.

0400 KEPT A SHARP LOOKOUT THROUGH THE WATCH.   2/0
0405 TESTED AUTO PILOT SYS. TO HAND & NFU MODE. FOUND IN GOOD
0420 ROUND MADE ALL ACC. & E/R AREA FOR SAFETY & FIRE & SECURITY. ALL'S WELL

0800 KEPT A SHARP LOOK OUT THROUGH THE WATCH.   2/0
0805 TESTED AUTO PILOT SYS. TO HAND & NFU MODE. FOUND IN GOOD.
0830 CHECKED RF CNTR'S TEMP. & CONDITION. ALL'S WELL.
0900 CHECKED LASHING CONDITION. RETAIGHTED LASHING MATERIALS OF ALL BAYS. ALL'S WELL.

1200 KEPT A SHARP LOOK OUT THROUGH THE WATCH.   3/O (M)
1205 TESTED AUTO PILOT SYS TO HAND & N.F.U. MODE FOUND IN GOOD.

(1300-1400) CONDUCTED SHIPBOARD EDUCATION FOR ALL CREWS AS BELOW. ALL CREW AWARE OF IT
   1) BIO-FOULING REGULATION.
   2) VGP (VESSEL GENERAL PERMIT) RULES.
   3) CBP & US PORT REGULATION TO BE OBSERVED

(1400-1500). C/O EDUCATED ALL DECK OFFICERS ABOUT BALLAST WATER MANAGEMENT & EXCHANGE ALL
   DECK OFFICERS UNDERSTOOD WELL.

1550 CHECKED CONDITION OF RF CNTRS. FOUND ALL IN GOOD.
1600 KEPT A SHARP LOOKOUT THROUGH THE WATCH.   2/0
1605 TESTED AUTOPILOT SYS. TO HAND & NFU MODE. FOUND IN GOOD.

2000 KEPT A SHARP LOOKOUT THRU THE WATCH.   3/O (M)
2005 TESTED AUTO PILOT SYS. TO HAND & NFU MODE. FOUND IN GOOD.

2100 ADVANCED ALL SHIP'S CLOCK 1HR TO MEET ZD: +11.0

2400 KEPT A SHARP LOOK OUT THROUGH THE WATCH.   3/O (A)

| Ch. Officer | | Master | |

참 고 문 헌

김성준, 『해사영어의 어원』, 문현출판, 2015.

박진수 · 김현종, 『**IMO 표준해사통신영어**』, 동원문화사, 2014.

이종인, 『현대해사영어(I)』, 효성출판사, 2000.

한국해양수산연수원, 『**GNDSS-GOC 교재**』, 동원문화사, 2016.

Boris Pritchard, *Maritime communications and IMO SMCP 2001* (Draft version), University of Rijeka, Croatia, 2003.

IMO Publication, *IMO SMCP with CD-ROM*, London UK, 2005.

IMO Res.A.918(22), *IMO Standard Marine Communication Phrases*, 2001.

IMO Res.A.954(23), *Proper Use of VHF Channels at Sea,* 2003.

Maritime and Coastguard Agency, MGN 324 (Radio: *Operational Guidance on the Use of VHF Radio and Automatic Identification Systems(AIS) at Sea*, Southampton UK, 2006.

P.C van Kluijven, *The International Maritime Language Programme*, Alk & Heijnen Publishers, The Netherlands, 2003.

Peter Trenkner, The *IMO Standard Maritime Communication Phrases in Dialogues*, Student course and Lecturer's course, 2016.

엮은이

❀ 박진수
한국해양대학교 항해학과(BSc), 동아대학교(MSc), 영국 Plymouth University(PhD)
한국해양대학교 실습선 선장(1급 항해사), 한국항해항만학회 회장 등 역임
현재 한국해양대학교 명예교수

❀ 김성준
한국해양대학교 항해학과(BSc), 고려대학교 문과대학 및 대학원(BA, MA, PhD)
목포해양대학교 조교수 역임, Master Mariner(STCW 95 II/2)
현재 한국해양대학교 항해융합학부 교수

Maritime English Communications based on
Standard Maritime Communication Practice

항 해 실 무 영 어

2021년 8월 25일 초판 인쇄
2021년 8월 30일 초판 발행

엮 은 이   박 진 수 · 김 성 준
펴 낸 이   한 신 규
본문디자인   안 혜 숙
표지디자인   이 은 영
펴 낸 곳   글터

주소 05827 서울특별시 송파구 동남로 11길 19(가락동)
전화 070 - 7613 - 9110 Fax02 - 443 - 0212 **E-mail** geul2013@naver.com
등록 2013년 4월 12일(제25100 - 2013 - 000041호)
출력 · 인쇄 ㈜대우인쇄 **제본** 보경문화사 **용지** 종이나무

ⓒ박진수 · 김성준, 2021
ⓒ글터, 2021, Printed in Korea

ISBN 979 - 11 - 88353 - 41 -5   93740   정가 19,000원